knit
edgings
& trims

THE HARMONY GUIDES

knit
edgings
& trims
150 stitches

edited by Kate Haxell

COLLINS & BROWN

C&B
CRAFTS

First published in the United Kingdom in 2009 by
Collins & Brown
10 Southcombe Street
London
W14 0RA

An imprint of Anova Books Company Ltd

ISBN 978-1-84340-524-5

A CIP catalogue for this book is available from the British Library.

9 8 7 6 5 4 3 2 1

Reproduction by Dot Gradations Ltd., UK
Printed and bound by 1010 Printing International Ltd,China

This book can be ordered direct from the publisher at
www.anovabooks.com.

contents

inspiration

From simple yet decorative ribs to intricate lace borders, there is an almost endless variety of edgings. They also offer a quick way of turning a plain knit garment into something supremely stylish.

This collection of 150 knitted edgings and trims takes its place in the new Harmony Guides and offers both the novice and master knitter a delicious selection of stitches to intrigue and inspire. As with all the Harmony Guides, this book is stitch-driven and concentrates on offering a diverse selection of patterns, chosen by knitters for knitters.

You'll find patterns for ribs, lace, appliqués, braids, inserts, borders, fringes, ruffles, cords and more, all just waiting to be tried out. Search for something specific or dip in to look for ideas and there's bound to be a pattern that catches your eye and makes your fingers itch to knit.

Attention to detail is a hallmark of all great designers, whatever the end product is that they make. In knitwear design it may be something as simple as a decorative rib that lifts a basic sweater pattern to a different level. A pretty flower appliqué can turn a plain beanie hat into a fashion statement, a delicate lace can lend extra glamour to a knitted silk camisole top or a beaded edge can give understated style to a garter stitch scarf. It really can be a tiny, easy-to-achieve element that makes your knitting extra special.

Like me, many knitters have some favourite patterns that fit and flatter and withstand the changing moods of fashion. We knit these patterns time and again, and sometimes even these favoured friends grow a little stale. In these pages you will find the solution – lovely edgings to give that great stocking stitch sweater, cosy scarf or moss stitch cushion a gorgeous burst of new style.

Often you will be able to simply add the edging to the existing pattern, but if you want a little more help or need to do some math to make the new trim fit the old pattern, you'll find helpful advice on page 19. It's rarely hard to combine an existing pattern with a fresh edging, so don't be put off trying any of the pieces in this book.

As most edgings are worked over just a few stitches, it's very quick, and doesn't take much yarn, to knit up a few centimetres to see how a pattern suits your project. So do take the time to consider different options from the many choices, and then pick the perfect one.

The small number of stitches makes lengthways edgings particularly attractive for novice knitters, who might turn pale at the idea of knitting a lace cardigan but can happily deal with a 12-stitch lace edge. To help those new to knitting, each edging has a stitch count whenever the number of stitches changes, so it's easy to keep track of where you are in the pattern and to quickly backtrack if you do make a mistake. The patterns have also been tested and checked, so you can knit them with confidence.

Whether you are knitting a project for a man, woman, child, home, or even your pooch, think about the way in which you can personalise it with a trim. An interesting rib pattern is an obvious – and very good – choice for a man's sweater, but would a narrow cable braid appeal? For a feminine woman there are myriad lace patterns to choose from, or maybe little shimmering beads or a soft leafy border would look fabulous.

When choosing patterns for babies, avoid lace and fur that little fingers can get caught in and look at perky points or tiny, sweet scallops instead. There are even choices for those most fashion-conscious of souls, teenage girls. Many of the vintage looks that continue to inspire catwalk fashion rely on fragile lace and decorative beading to make the most of the style.

If you are knitting accessories then you will positively revel in the possibilities open to you. Knitting a snuggly scarf for a friend? Don't just fringe the ends, fringe them with beads, add an extravagant ruffle or a stylish, contemporary lace band. Give sock tops a picot trim, mittens a bobbled rib cuff or a bag a scalloped top edge. Remember that braids can be stitched on to almost anything and range in style from cute heart patterns to textural designs that will work perfectly with modern shapes and styles.

Don't forget your interior projects when it comes to making these choices. Throws and afghans are stand-out choices for fancy borders, but cushions, runners and laundry bags will also benefit from the added detail that an edging can bring. A band of embossed diamonds will sit perfectly across the envelope back of a garter stitch cushion, or why be shy, work it as an insert across the front.

As long as you take into account any potential laundering issues, there's no reason why knitted trims can't be applied to cloth projects. This winter my much-loved, but rather elderly, wool fabric skirt got a new lace hem knitted in variegated mohair yarn: this gave it a great new look. Similarly, my stripy ticking tote bag looks fantastic with its new cotton knitted braid sewn on around the top edge.

Remember that any edging pattern will change its look, sometimes quite dramatically, depending on the yarn it is knitted in. Working a classic lace pattern in a 4-ply merino will give a pretty, retro result; the same pattern in supple silk will ooze glamour and knitted in a chunky yarn it can have a surprisingly contemporary look. Get out your needles and experiment – I hope you discover a new world of knitting choices and love it as much as I have.

tools & equipment

To master any skill, it's imperative to have the right equipment to work with. This section provides useful information that can come in handy while knitting.

Knitting Needles

Knitting needles are used in pairs to produce a flat, knitted fabric. They are pointed at one end to form the stitches and have a knob at the other to retain the stitches. Made in plastic, wood, steel or alloy, they range in size from 2mm in diameter upwards. In England, needles used to be sized by numbers; the higher the number, the smaller the needle. In America, the opposite is true – higher numbers mean larger sizes. Metric sizing has now been adopted in most countries.

Needles are also of different lengths to hold the stitches required for a project. Edgings worked lengthways use only a few stitches, so short needles are best; those worked from the bottom up or top down may need longer needles, depending on the length of edging you want to make.

A circular needle can be used to work very long bottom-up or top-down edgings. This is two needle points joined by a plastic cord and they come in varying lengths. Usually used for knitting in the round to produce tubes, you can also knit back and forth on them to produce wide, flat fabric.

It is useful to have a range of sizes so that tension swatches can be knitted up and compared. Discard any needles that become bent. Points should be fairly sharp, as blunt needles reduce the speed and ease of working.

Double-pointed needles are used to produce I-cords, which make perfect drawstrings, handles for bags and can be sewn on as decorative edgings in their own right. Double-pointed needles are sold in sets of four or five.

Cable needles are short needles used to hold the stitches of a cable to the back or front of the main body of knitting.

Other Useful Equipment

Needle gauges are punched with holes corresponding to the needle sizes and are marked with both the old numerical sizing and the metric sizing, so you can easily check the size of any needle.

Stitch holders resemble large safety pins and are used to hold stitches while they are not being worked. As an alternative, thread a blunt-pointed sewing needle with a generous length of contrast-coloured yarn, thread it through the stitches to be held while they are still on the needle, then slip the stitches off the needle and knot both ends of the contrast yarn to secure the stitches.

Wool sewing needles or tapestry needles are used to sew completed pieces of knitting together. They are large, with a broad eye for easy threading and a blunt point that will slip between the knitted stitches without splitting and fraying the yarn. Do not use sharp-pointed sewing needles to sew up knitting.

A row counter is a cylinder with a numbered dial that is used to count the number of rows that have been knitted. Push it onto the needle and turn the dial at the end of each row. This is very useful for keeping track of where you are in intricate lace edging patterns.

A tape measure is essential for checking tension swatches and for measuring lengthways edgings as you work them. For an accurate result, always smooth the knitting (without stretching it) on a firm flat surface before measuring it.

A crochet hook is useful for picking up dropped stitches.

Knitting Yarn

Yarn is the term used for strands of spun fibre that are twisted together into a continuous length of the required thickness. Yarn can be of animal origin (wool, angora, mohair, silk, alpaca), vegetable origin (cotton, linen, bamboo, soya), or man-made (nylon, acrylic, rayon). Yarn may be made up from a combination of different fibres.

Each single strand of knitting yarn is known as a ply. A number of plys are twisted together to form the yarn. The texture and characteristics of the yarn may be varied by the combination of fibres and by the way in which the yarn is spun. Wool and other natural fibres are often combined with man-made fibres to make a yarn that is more economical and hard-wearing. Wool can also be treated to make it machine washable. The twist of this yarn is firm and smooth and knits up into a hard-wearing fabric. Loosely twisted yarn has a softer finish when knitted.

Buying Yarn

Yarn is most commonly sold in balls of specific weight measured in grams or ounces. Some yarn, particularly very thick yarn, is also sold in a coiled hank or skein that must be wound into a ball before you can begin knitting with it.

Yarn manufacturers (called spinners) wrap each ball with a paper band on which is printed a lot of necessary information. The ball band states the weight of the yarn and its composition. It will give instructions for washing and ironing and will state the ideal range of needle sizes to be used with the yarn. The ball band also carries the shade number and dye lot number. It is important that you use yarn of the same dye lot for an entire project. Different dye lots vary subtly in shading; this may not be apparent when you are holding the two balls, but it will show as a variation in shade on the finished piece of knitting.

Always keep the ball band as a reference. The best way is to pin it to the tension swatch (see page 17) and keep them together with any leftover yarn and spare buttons or other trimmings. That way, you can always check the washing instructions and also have materials for repairs.

the basics

Once you have mastered the basics of knitting, you can go on to develop your skills and start making more challenging projects.

Casting On

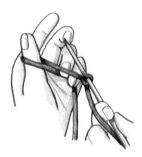

1 Make a slip knot 1m (39in) from the end of the yarn. Hold the needle in your right hand, with the ball end of the yarn over your index finger. Wind the loose end of the yarn around your left thumb from front to back.

2 *Insert the point of the needle under the first strand of yarn on your thumb.

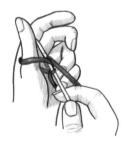

3 With your right index finger, take the ball end of the yarn over the point of the needle.

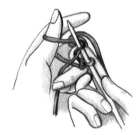

4 Pull a loop through to form the first stitch. Remove your left thumb from the yarn. Pull the loose end to secure the stitch. Repeat from * until all stitches have been cast on.

Knit Stitch

1 Hold the needle with the cast-on stitches in your left hand, with the loose yarn at the back of the work. Insert the right-hand needle from left to right through the front of the first stitch on the left-hand needle.

2 Wind the yarn from left to right over the point of the right-hand needle.

3 Draw the yarn through the stitch, thus forming a new stitch on the right-hand needle.

4 Slip the original stitch off the left-hand needle, keeping the new stitch on the right-hand needle.

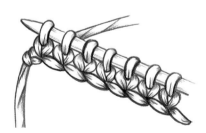

5 To knit a row, repeat steps 1 to 4 until all the stitches have been transferred from the left-hand needle to the right-hand needle. Turn the work, transferring the needle that holds the stitches to your left hand to work the next row.

Purl Stitch

1 Hold the needle with the stitches in your left hand with the loose yarn at the front of the work. Insert the right-hand needle from right to left into the front of the first stitch on the left-hand needle.

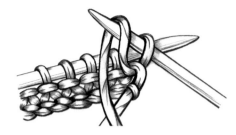

2 Wind the yarn from right to left over the point of the right-hand needle.

3 Draw the yarn through the stitch, thus forming a new stitch on the right-hand needle.

4 Slip the original stitch off the left-hand needle, keeping the new stitch on the right-hand needle.

5 To purl a row, repeat steps 1 to 4 until all the stitches have been transferred from the left-hand needle to the right-hand needle. Turn the work as for knit stitch.

Increasing

The simplest method of increasing one stitch is to work into the front and back of the same stitch.

On a knit row, knit into the front of the stitch to be increased into; then, before slipping it off the needle, place the right-hand needle behind the left-hand needle and knit again into the back of the same stitch. Slip the original stitch off the left-hand needle.

On a purl row, purl into the front of the stitch to be increased into; then, before slipping it off the needle, purl again into the back of the same stitch. Slip the original stitch off the left-hand needle.

Decreasing

The simplest method of decreasing one stitch is to work two stitches together.

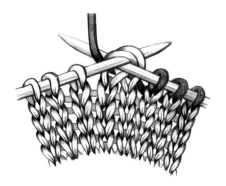

On a knit row, insert the right-hand needle from left to right through two stitches instead of one, then knit them together as one stitch. This is called knit two together (k2tog).

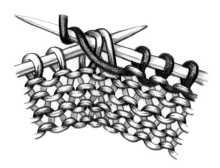

On a purl row, insert the right-hand needle from right to left through two stitches instead of one, then purl them together as one stitch. This is called purl two together (p2tog).

Casting Off

There is one simple, most commonly used method of securing stitches once you have finished a piece of knitting – casting off. The cast-off edge should always have the same 'give' or elasticity as the fabric and you should always cast off in the stitch pattern used for the main fabric unless the pattern directs otherwise.

Knitwise

Knit two stitches. *Using the point of the left-hand needle, lift the first stitch on the right-hand needle over the second then drop it off the needle. Knit the next stitch and repeat from * until all stitches have been worked off the left-hand needle and only one stitch remains on the right-hand needle. Cut the yarn (leaving enough to sew in the end), thread the end through the stitch, and then slip it off the needle. Draw the yarn up firmly to fasten off.

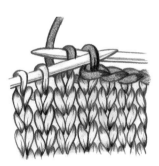

Purlwise

Purl two stitches. *Using the point of the left-hand needle, lift the first stitch on the right-hand needle over the second and drop it off the needle. Purl the next stitch and repeat from * until all the stitches have been worked off the left-

hand needle and only one stitch remains on the right-hand needle. Secure the last stitch in the same way as described for casting off knitwise.

Tension

The information given under this heading at the beginning of all patterns refers to the number of stitches required to fill a particular area; for example, a frequent tension indication would be '22 sts and 30 rows = 10cm (4in) square measured over stocking stitch on 4mm needles'. This means that, in order to obtain the correct measurements for the garment you intend to knit, you need to produce fabric made up of the proportion of stitches and rows given in the tension paragraph, regardless of the needles you use. The needle size indicated in the pattern is the one that most knitters will use to achieve this tension, but it is the tension that is important, not the needle size.

The way to ensure that you do achieve the correct tension is to work a tension sample or swatch before starting the main part of the knitting. Although this may seem to be a waste of time and a nuisance, it can save the enormous amount of time and aggravation that would result from having knitted a garment the wrong size.

The correct tension is as important in knitting an edging as it is in knitting a garment. Usually you will be knitting the edging in the same yarn as the garment, so the same needles should be fine. However, depending on the edging pattern you choose, you may need to change needle size, usually going to one or more sizes larger.

Tension Swatch

If you are working a lengthways edging, then work the pattern to make a tension swatch that measures at least 15cm (6in) or three pattern repeats in length. Cast the swatch off loosely. You should now be able to judge visually whether the needle size is correct. Does the edging look like the photograph that accompanies the pattern? Does it lie flat and drape well? If you can't see the design of the edging clearly, or it curls up and is stiff, then try another swatch using a larger needle. However, if the edging is loose and baggy and the swatch is floppy with an insubstantial edge, then try again using a smaller needle.

If you are planning to use an edge that is knitted from the bottom up or top down, then work it as part of your garment tension swatch before you start the project.

The instructions given in the tension paragraph of a knitting pattern will be either for working in stocking stitch or in a pattern stitch. If they are given in a pattern stitch, you need to cast on a multiple of stitches for the edging (see page 19) that adds up to the same number as is required for the pattern stitch. If the swatch is in stocking stitch, any multiple that suits the edging pattern can be used. Whichever method is used, the fabric should always be at least 12cm (5in) wide.

For a bottom-up edging swatch, work the edging then the rest of the swatch in pattern or stocking stitch until the piece measures at least 15cm (6in) in depth. Break the yarn about 15cm (6in) from the work and thread this end through the stitches, then remove the knitting needle. For a top-down edging, work the fabric then the edging, then cast off as described in the edging instructions.

Place a pin vertically into the fabric a few stitches from the side edge. Measure 10cm (4in) carefully and insert a second pin. Count the stitches between the pins. If the number of stitches is less than that specified in the pattern (even by one stitch), your garment will be too large. Use smaller needles and knit another tension sample. If your sample has more stitches over 10cm (4in), the garment will be too small. Change to larger needles. In the same way, check the number of rows against the given tension, too.

Unless the edging is a rib or another pattern that is designed to draw in the fabric, the edging should lie flat across the end of your swatch. If it draws the fabric in, then work another swatch using a larger needle for the edging and changing back to the needle size given in the pattern for the knitted fabric. If the edging flares out, then try again using a smaller needle for that section.

It is most important to get the width measurement correct before starting to knit. Length measurements can usually be adjusted during the course of the knitting by adjusting the measurement to underarm or the sleeve length, which is frequently given as a measurement and not in rows. Remember that if you are adding an edging to a cuff or hem then you may need to re-calculate the number of rows so that the sleeve or garment is not too long.

Stitch Counts and Multiples

If an edging is worked lengthways then the instruction at the start of the pattern will say, for example, 'Worked lengthways over 10 sts'. This means that you cast on 10 stitches to work the first row. Once you have worked all the pattern rows, you simply repeat them until the edging is the required length.

The instructions may tell you to finish the final repeat on a particular row. This is usually so that if the ends of the knitted edging are joined to form a circle, the pattern will run as evenly as possible across the join. If a particular row is not given, end the last repeat with the last pattern row.

Depending on the pattern, the number of stitches on the needle may vary on rows. When the number changes, a stitch count is given in brackets at the end of the row. This count includes all loops on the needle, whether they are full stitches or yarnovers. If no stitch count is given then the number of stitches has not changed since the last count. So, a lengthways pattern with no stitch counts at all has the same number of stitches on every row as originally cast on.

Some patterns need a foundation row that does not form part of the repeat. These are marked as such in the patterns.

Edgings that are worked from the top down or bottom up have different instructions. The 'multiple' or repeat of the pattern is given at the start – for example, 'Starts with multiple of 7 sts + 4 sts'. This means you can cast on any number of stitches that is a multiple of 7, plus 4 balancing stitches – for instance, 14 + 4, 21 + 4, 28 + 4, and so on. These patterns obviously do not have stitch counts at the ends of the rows, so you will need to follow the increases and decreases carefully to keep the pattern correct.

The number of times the pattern rows need to be repeated to make the edging shown in the swatch will be specified, though on many of the patterns you could work the repeat more often to create a deeper edging if required.

If you are going to work a bottom-up edging and then continue knitting the project, you need to make sure that the number of stitches the edging finishes with – for example, 'Ends with multiple of 6 sts + 2 sts' – can be multiplied to make the correct number of stitches for the first row of the project. So, the first row of the project needs to be any multiple of 6 stitches, plus 2 balancing stitches.

For a top-down edging worked on the lower edge of a project, check the multiple the edging starts with. Edging patterns won't work without the correct multiple, so you will usually need to adjust the number of project stitches.

However, if the number of project stitches is just one or two more than is needed for the edging, then you can add one or two selvedge stitches to the end of the edging pattern, but remember they are there and don't try to work them into the pattern. Make careful notes of any changes and consider how they might affect other areas of the project.

Of course, both bottom-up and top-down edgings can be worked as strips and sewn on afterwards if preferred.

Attaching edgings

Lengthways edgings need to be sewn to the finished project. Usually it is best to use a tapestry needle and matching yarn and whip stitch the top edge of the edging to the knitted fabric. To attach an edging to cloth fabric, use a sewing needle and matching sewing thread.

stitch gallery

Leaf Edging

Worked lengthways over 8 sts.

Note: increases are worked purlwise.

1st row (right side): K5, yo, k1, yo, k2. (10 sts)

2nd row: P6, inc, k3. (11 sts)

3rd row: K4, p1, k2, yo, k1, yo, k3. (13 sts)

4th row: P8, inc, k4. (14 sts)

5th row: K4, p2, k3, yo, k1, yo, k4. (16 sts)

6th row: P10, inc, k5. (17 sts)

7th row: K4, p3, k4, yo, k1, yo, k5. (19 sts)

8th row: P12, inc, k6. (20 sts)

9th row: K4, p4, yb, skpo, k7, k2tog, k1. (18 sts)

10th row: P10, inc, k7. (19 sts)

11th row: K4, p5, yb, skpo, k5, k2tog, k1. (17 sts)

12th row: P8, inc, k2, p1, k5. (18 sts)

13th row: K4, p1, k1, p4, yb, skpo, k3, k2tog, k1. (16 sts)

14th row: P6, inc, k3, p1, k5. (17 sts)

15th row: K4, p1, k1, p5, yb, skpo, k1, k2tog, k1. (15 sts)

16th row: P4, inc, k4, p1, k5. (16 sts)

17th row: K4, p1, k1, p6, yb, sk2po, k1. (14 sts)

18th row: P2tog, cast off 5 sts purlwise using p2tog as first of these sts, k1, p1, k5. (8 sts)

Rep these 18 rows.

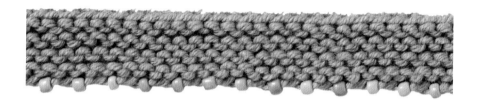

Beaded Thumb Cast On

Worked from bottom edge upwards.

Starts and ends with multiple of 2 sts + 1 st.

Note: Thread beads onto knitting yarn before casting on, 1 bead for each alt st, less 2, to give a selvedge st at each end.

Leaving a tail of yarn long enough for the required number of sts to be cast on, make a slip knot in the yarn above the threaded beads and place this on the needle.

Cast on 1 st.

*Slide 1 bead up against the needle before looping the yarn around the thumb to cast on next st.

Cast on 1 st.

Rep from * until 1 less than required number of sts are on LH needle.

Cast on 1 st.

This forms the edging.

Cont as required. Usually the 1st row will be a wrong side row to show the beads to best effect.

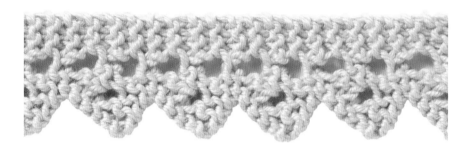

Trefoil Bunting

Worked lengthways over 5 sts.

1st row (right side): K3, yo2, k2. (7 sts)
2nd row: K3, p1, k3.
Work 2 rows in garter stitch.
5th row: K3, yo2, k2tog, yo2, k2. (10 sts)
6th row: K3, p1, k2, p1, k3.
7th row: Knit.
8th row: Cast off 5 sts, k4. (5 sts)
Rep these 8 rows.

Box Pleats

Worked from bottom edge upwards.

Starts with multiple of 24 sts.

Ends with multiple of 8 sts.

Note: Cast on using the cable method. Slip all sts purlwise. Slipping the st wyf (with yarn in front) makes a back fold: slipping the st wyb (with yarn at back) makes a front fold.

1st row (right side): K4, *sl 1 wyf, k3, sl 1 wyb, k6, sl 1 wyb, k3, sl 1 wyf, k8; rep from *, ending k4.

2nd row: Purl.

Rep 1st and 2nd rows 5 more times.

13th row (join pleats): *[Slip next 4 sts onto a double-pointed needle] twice, fold fabric on columns of slip sts so that LH needle and double-pointed needles are parallel and fold is at the back and k 1 st from each needle tog 4 times; rep from *, folding into box pleats.

14th and 15th rows: Knit.

These 15 rows form the edging.

Cast off or cont as required

Cast-off Fringe

Worked lengthways over 3 sts.

Note: cast on using the cable method.

1st to 3rd rows: Sl 1, k2.

4th row (wrong side): Cast on 6 sts, cast off 6 sts, k2. (3 sts)

Rep these 4 rows, ending with a 3rd row.

Twist Edge

Worked from bottom edge upwards.

Starts and ends with a multiple of 6 sts.

Note: cast on using the thumb method.

Starting with a k row, work 6 rows st st.

7th row (right side): *K6, take the tip of the LH needle under the cast on edge to the back of the work and around to the working position again; rep from *, ending k6.

These 7 rows form the edging.

Cont as required.

Butterfly Edging

Worked lengthways over 8 sts.

1st row (right side): Sl 1, k2, yo, k2tog yo2, k2tog, k1. (9 sts)

2nd row: K3, p1, k2, yo, k2tog, k1.

3rd row: Sl 1, k2, yo, k2tog, k1, yo2, k2tog, k1. (10 sts)

4th row: K3, p1, k3, yo, k2tog, k1.

5th row: Sl 1, k2, yo, k2tog, k2, yo2, k2tog, k1. (11 sts)

6th row: K3, p1, k4, yo, k2tog, k1.

7th row: Sl 1, k2, yo, k2tog, k6.

8th row: Cast off 3 sts, k4, yo, k2tog, k1. (8 sts)

Rep these 8 rows.

Arrow Braid

Worked lengthways over 9 sts.

Triangles
Put a slip knot on the needle.

1st row (right side): Inc. (2 sts)

2nd row: Inc, k1. (3 sts)

3rd row: Inc, k2. (4 sts)

4th row: Inc, k3. (5 sts)

5th row: Inc, k4. (6 sts)

6th row: Inc, k5. (7 sts)

7th row: Inc, k6. (8 sts)

8th row: Inc, k7. (9 sts)

Cut yarn and leave sts on spare needle. Rep these 8 rows to make as many triangles as required.

Band
Cast on 9 sts.

1st to 6th rows: Sl 1, k8.

7th row (right side): Slip 9 sts of one triangle onto cable needle and, right side facing, hold in front of needle with band and k 1 st from each needle tog across the row.

8th row: Sl 1, k8.

Rep these 8 rows, ending with a 6th row.

Moss and Faggot

Worked lengthways over 17 sts.

1st row (right side): K2, yo, k3, yo, k2tog, [p1, k1] 5 times. (18 sts)

2nd row: [K1, p1] 4 times, k1, k2tog, yo, k5, yo, k2. (19 sts)

3rd row: K2, yo, k1, k2tog, yo, k1, yo, k2tog, k1, yo, k2tog, [p1, k1] 4 times. (20 sts)

4th row: [K1, p1] 3 times, k1, [k2tog, yo, k1] twice, k2, yo, k2tog, k1, yo, k2. (21 sts)

5th row: K2, yo, k1, k2tog, yo, k5, yo, k2tog, k1, yo, k2tog, [p1, k1] 3 times. (22 sts)

6th row: [K1, p1] twice, k1, [k2tog, yo, k1] twice, k6, yo, k2tog, k1, yo, k2. (23 sts)

7th row: [K2tog, k1, yo] twice, k2tog, k3, [k2tog, yo, k1] twice, [p1, k1] 3 times. (22 sts)

8th row: [K1, p1] 4 times, yo, k2tog, k1, yo, k2tog, [k1, k2tog, yo] twice, k1, k2tog. (21 sts)

9th row: [K2tog, k1, yo] twice, k3tog, yo, k1, k2tog, yo, [k1, p1] 4 times, k1. (20 sts)

10th row: [K1, p1] 5 times, yo, k2tog, k3, k2tog, yo, k1, k2tog. (19 sts)

11th row: K2tog, k1, yo, k2tog, k1, k2tog, yo, [k1, p1] 5 times, k1. (18 sts)

12th row: [K1, p1] 6 times, yo, k3tog, yo, k1, k2tog. (17 sts)

Rep these 12 rows.

Ladder Braid

Worked lengthways over 11 sts.

1st row (right side): Sl 1, k10.
2nd row: Sl 1, k1, p7, k2.
Rep 1st and 2nd rows once more.
5th row: Sl 1, k1, p7, k2.
6th row: As 2nd row.
7th row: As 1st row.
Rep 6th and 7th rows once more.
10th row: Sl 1, k10.
Rep these 10 rows.

Moss Stitch Cord

Worked lengthways over 5 sts on double-pointed needles.

1st row: K1, *p1, k1; rep from * to end, do not turn, slide sts to other end of needle.
2nd row: P1, *k1, p1; rep from * to end, do not turn, slide sts to other end of needle.
Rep these 2 rows.

Lace and Bobble

Worked from bottom edge upwards.

Starts and ends with multiple of 10 sts + 1 st.

Note: cast on using the thumb method.

Special abbreviation: MB = make bobble. (P1, k1, p1) in next st, turn, k1, p1, k1, turn, p1, k1, p1, pass 2nd and 3rd sts over 1st st.

1st row (wrong side): *P5, MB, p4; rep from *, ending last rep p5.

2nd row: K1, *yo, k3, sk2po, k3, yo, k1; rep from * to end.

3rd row: Purl.

4th row: P1, *k1, yo, k2, sk2po, k2, yo, k1, p1; rep from * to end.

5th row: *K1, p9; rep from *, ending last rep k1.

6th row: P1, *k2, yo, k1, sk2po, k1, yo, k2, p1; rep from * to end.

7th row: As 5th row.

8th row: P1, *k3, yo, sk2po, yo, k3, p1; rep from * to end.

9th row: Purl.

10th row: K1, *k3, yo, sk2po, yo, k4; rep from * to end.

11th row: Purl.

Rep 10th and 11th rows once more.

These 13 rows form the edging.

Cast off or cont as required.

Snail Shell Lace

Worked lengthways over 19 sts.

Foundation row: Knit.

1st row (wrong side): K5, p1, yo, p2tog, k8, yo, k2tog, k1.

2nd row: K3, yo, k2tog, k5, k2tog, yo, k1, yo, ssk, k2, yo2, k2. (21 sts)

3rd row: K3, p1, k1, p2tog tbl, yo, p3, yo, p2tog, k6, yo, k2tog, k1.

4th row: K3, yo, k2tog, k3, k2tog, yo, k2, k2tog, yo, k1, yo, ssk, k2, yo2, k2. (23 sts)

5th row: K3, p1, k1, p2tog tbl, yo, p3, yo, p2tog, p2, yo, p2tog, k4, yo, k2tog, k1.

6th row: K3, yo, k2tog, k1, [k2tog, yo, k2] twice, yo, ssk, k1, yo, ssk, k2, yo2, k2. (25 sts)

7th row: K3, p1, k1, [p2tog tbl, yo, p1] twice, yo, p2tog, p1, yo, p2tog, p2, yo, p2tog, k2, yo, k2tog, k1.

8th row: K3, yo, k3tog, yo, k2, k2tog, yo, k1, k2tog, yo, k3, yo, ssk, k1, yo, ssk, k2tog, yo2, k2tog.

9th row: K2, p1, k1, p2, yo, p2tog, p1, yo, p3tog, yo, p1, p2tog tbl, yo, p2, p2tog tbl, yo, k3, yo, k2tog, k1.

10th row: K3, yo, k2tog, [k2, yo, ssk] twice, k3, k2tog, yo, k2, sk2po, yo2, k2tog. (24 sts)

11th row: K2, p5, yo, p2tog, p1, p2tog tbl, yo, p2, p2tog tbl, yo, k5, yo, k2tog, k1.

12th row: K3, yo, k2tog, k4, yo, ssk, k2, yo, k3tog, yo, k2, k3tog, yo, k2tog, k1. (22 sts)

13th row: K3, p1, k3, yo, p2tog, p1, p2tog tbl, yo, k7, yo, k2tog, k1.

14th row: K3, yo, k2tog, k6, yo, k3tog, yo, k2, k3tog, yo, k3tog. (19 sts)

Rep 1st to 14th rows.

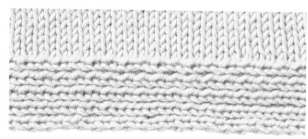

Wavy Border

Worked lengthways over 13 sts.

1st and every alt row (wrong side): K2, p to last 2 sts, k2.
2nd row: K4, yo, k5, yo, k2tog, yo, k2. (15 sts)
4th row: K5, sk2po, k2, [yo, k2tog] twice, k1. (13 sts)
6th row: K4, skpo, k2, [yo, k2tog] twice, k1. (12 sts)
8th row: K3, skpo, k2, [yo, k2tog] twice, k1. (11 sts)
10th row: K2, skpo, k2, [yo, k2tog] twice, k1. (10 sts)
12th row: K1, skpo, k2, yo, k1, yo, k2tog, yo, k2. (11 sts)
14th row: K4, yo, k3, yo, k2tog, yo, k2. (13 sts)
Rep these 14 rows.

Horizontal Rib

Worked from bottom edge upwards.

Worked over any odd number of sts for required depth of rib.

Note: 1 st can be picked up from each row end of the rib band for a fuller fabric. If a flatter fabric is required, skip every 4th row end when picking up. Stitch counts will need to be calculated accordingly.

1st row (right side): K1, *p1, k1; rep from * to end.
2nd row: P1, *k1, p1; rep from * to end.
Rep these 2 rows until rib band is required length and cast off.

Pick up sts (see note above) along one side edge and cont as required.

Fern Lace

Worked lengthways over 14 sts.

1st row (right side): Sl 1, k2, [yo, k2tog] twice, k1, yo2, [k2tog] twice, yo, k2. (15 sts)

2nd row: K5, [k1, p1] twice in yo2, k8. (17 sts)

3rd row: Sl 1, k3, [yo, k2tog] twice, k5, k2tog, yo, k2.

4th and every alt row: Knit.

5th row: Sl 1, k4, [yo, k2tog] twice, k4, k2tog, yo, k2.

7th row: Sl 1, k5, [yo, k2tog] twice, k3, k2tog, yo, k2.

9th row: Sl 1, k6, [yo, k2tog] twice, k2, k2tog, yo, k2.

11th row: Sl 1, k7, [yo, k2tog] twice, k1, k2tog, yo, k2.

13th row: Sl 1, k8, [yo, k2tog] twice, k2tog, yo, k2.

15th row: Sl 1, k9, [yo, k2tog] twice, k1, yo, k2. (18 sts)

17th row: Sl 1, k10, yo, [k2tog] twice, sl last st back onto LH needle, 1 at a time, lift next 3 sts over it then replace st on RH needle. (14 sts)

18th row: Knit.

Rep these 18 rows, ending with a 17th row.

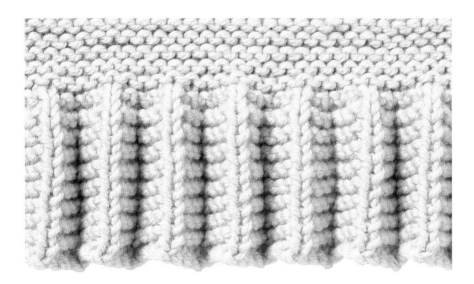

Accordion Pleat

Worked from bottom edge upwards.

Starts with twice the number of sts needed that is a multiple of 8 sts.

Ends with multiple of 8 sts.

Note: cast on using the thumb method.

1st row (right side): *K7, p1; rep from * to end.

2nd row: K4, *p1, k7; rep from * to last 4 sts, p1, k3.

Rep 1st and 2nd rows as required, ending with a 2nd row.

Next row: [K2tog] to end.

These rows form the edging.

Cast off or cont as required.

Thick and Thin Rib

Worked from bottom edge upwards.

Starts and ends with multiple of 8 sts + 6 sts.

Note: cast on using the thumb method.

1st row (right side): K6, *p2, k6; rep from * to end.

2nd row: P6, *k2, p6; rep from * to end.

Rep 1st and 2nd rows twice more.

7th row: K2, *p2, k2; rep from * to end.

8th row: P2, *k2, p2; rep from * to end.

Rep 7th and 8th rows twice more.

13th row: K2, p2, *k6, p2; rep from * to last 2 sts, k2.

14th row: P2, k2, *p6, k2; rep from * to last 2 sts, p2.

Rep 13th and 14th rows twice more.

These 18 rows form the edging.

Cast off or cont as required.

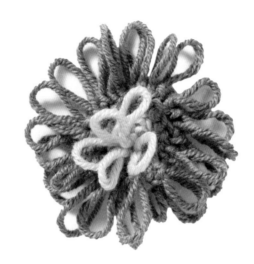

Perforated Rib

Worked from bottom edge upwards.

Starts and ends with multiple of 4 sts + 1 st.

Note: cast on using the thumb method.

1st row (right side): K1, *p3, k1; rep from * to end.
2nd row: P1, *k3, p1; rep from * to end.
Rep 1st and 2nd rows once more.
5th row: K1, *p2tog, yo, p1, k1; rep from * to end.
6th row: As 2nd row.
Rep 1st to 6th rows once more then the 1st to 4th rows once more.
These 16 rows form the edging.
Cast off or cont as required.

Loop Flower Appliqué

Note: two colours of yarn are used, A and B.
With A, cast on 27 sts.

1st row (right side): ML in every st.
2nd row: K2tog to last st, k1. (14 sts)
Change to B.
3rd row: ML in first five sts, k2tog to last st, k1. (10 sts)
4th row: [K2tog] twice, *pass 1st st over 2nd st, k2tog; rep from * twice more, pass 1st st over 2nd st, fasten off.
Coil up with B loops in centre, loops facing inwards.
Sew coil together around base.

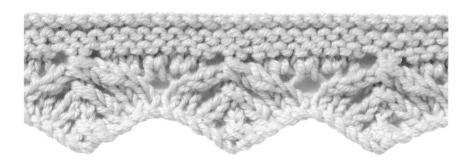

Scallop Lace Edging

Worked from bottom edge upwards.

Starts with multiple of 13 sts + 2 sts.

Ends with multiple of 10 sts + 3 sts.

Note: cast on using the thumb method.

1st row (right side): K3, *skpo, sl 2, k3tog, p2sso, k2tog, k4; rep from * to last 12 sts, skpo, sl 2, k3tog, p2sso, k2tog, k3.

2nd row: P4, *yo, p1, yo, p6; rep from * to last 5 sts, yo, p1, yo, p4.

3rd row: K1, yo, *k2, skpo, k1, k2tog, k2, yo; rep from * to last st, k1.

4th row: P2, *yo, p2, yo, p3, yo, p2, yo, p1; rep from * to last st, p1.

5th row: K2, yo, k1, *yo, skpo, k1, sk2po, k1, k2tog, [yo, k1] 3 times; rep from * to last 12 sts, yo, skpo, k1, sk2po, k1, k2tog, yo, k1, yo, k2.

6th row: Purl.

7th row: K5, *yo, sl 2, k3tog, p2sso, yo, k7; rep from * to last 10 sts, yo, sl 2, k3tog, p2sso, yo, k5.

Work 4 rows in garter st.

These 11 rows form the edging.

Cast off or cont as required

Tags

Worked lengthways over 4 sts.

1st row (wrong side): Sl 1, k3.
2nd to 4th rows: As 1st row.
5th row: Cast on 3 sts, k all 7 sts. (7 sts)
6th to 10th rows: Sl 1, k6.
11th row: Cast off 3 sts, k3. (4 sts)
12th to 18th rows: Sl 1, k3.
Rep the 5th to 18th rows, ending with a 15th row.

Beaded Frill

Worked from bottom edge upwards.

Starts with twice the number of sts required + 1 st.

Note: Thread beads onto knitting yarn before casting on, 1 bead for each alt st.

Cast on using Beaded Thumb Cast On (see page 23), omitting the selvedge sts.

1st row (wrong side): Purl.

2nd row: [K2tog] to last st, k1.

These 2 rows form the edging.

Cont as required.

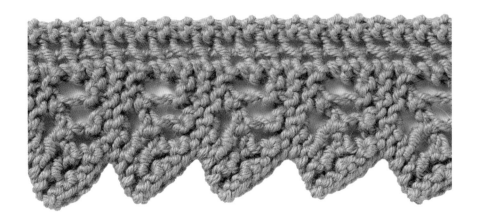

Willow Edging

Worked lengthways over 10 sts.

1st row (right side): Sl 1, k2, yo, k2tog, *yo2, k2tog; rep from * once more, k1. (12 sts)

2nd row: K3, [p1, k2] twice, yo, k2tog, k1.

3rd row: Sl 1, k2, yo, k2tog, k2, *yo2, k2tog; rep from * once more, k1. (14 sts)

4th row: K3, p1, k2, p1, k4, yo, k2tog, k1.

5th row: Sl 1, k2, yo, k2tog, k4, *yo2, k2tog; rep from * once more, k1. (16 sts)

6th row: K3, p1, k2, p1, k6, yo, k2tog, k1.

7th row: Sl 1, k2, yo, k2tog, k11.

8th row: Cast off 6 sts, k6, yo, k2tog, k1. (10 sts)

Rep these 8 rows.

Scalloped Ruffle

Worked from bottom edge upwards.

Starts with multiple of 11 sts + 2 sts.

Ends with multiple of 2 sts.

Note: cast on using the thumb method.

1st row (wrong side): Purl.

2nd row: K2, *k1, sl st back onto LH needle, with RH needle, 1 at a time, lift next 8 sts over this st and off needle, yo2, k first st again, k2; rep from * to end.

3rd row: K1, *p2tog, drop first loop of yo2, [k1, p1] twice in second loop, p1; rep from *, ending k1.

4th row: *K4, yo, k2tog; rep from * to last 2 sts, k2.

5th row: Purl.

Rep 4th and 5th rows twice more.

10th row: K2, *k2tog, k1; rep from * to end.

Work 3 rows in garter stitch.

These 13 rows form the edging.

Cast off or cont as required.

Buttoned Tags

Worked from bottom edge upwards.

Starts and ends with multiple of 7 sts.

Note: cast on using the thumb method. Each tag is worked separately and then joined on one row. Tags can be same length or, as here, different lengths.

Cast on 7 sts.

1st row (right side): K1, [p1, k1] three times.

Rep 1st row 6 more times.

8th row: K1, p1, k1, yo, k2tog, p1, k1.

Rep 1st row as required, ending with a wrong side row. These rows form one tag. Cut yarn and leave finished tag on needle. On the same needle, cast on 7 sts and work 2nd tag.

Cont in this way until there are as many tags as required.

Join tags

Do not cut yarn after completing the last tag.

Next row (right side): K1, [p1, k1] three times, *cast on 3 sts, k1, [p1, k1] three times across next tag; rep from * until all tags are joined.

Next row: K1, *p1, k1; rep from * to end.

Rep last row 5 more times.

These rows form the edging.

Cast off or cont as required.

Sew buttons to fabric above tags and slip eyelets over buttons.

Beaded Cast Off

Note: before casting off, measure out a length of yarn 4 times the width of the knitted fabric. Cut yarn. Thread on beads, 1 bead for every alt st.

Cast off 1 st.
*Slide a bead up to sit behind the st, insert RH needle knitwise into next st and knit, drawing bead through on stitch loop. Lift 1st loop on RH needle over 2nd loop.
Cast off 1 st.
Rep from *, fastening off last st.

Smocked Rib

Worked from bottom edge upwards.

Starts and ends with multiple of 6 sts + 3 sts.

Special abbreviations: S3 = smock 3. Yb, sl next 3 sts purlwise, yf, sl same 3 sts back onto LH needle, yb, sl same 3 sts back to RH needle.

Note: cast on using the thumb method.

1st and 3rd rows (right side): P3, *k3, p3; rep from * to end.

2nd and every alt row: K3, *p3, k3; rep from * to end.

5th row: P3, *S3, p3; rep from * to end.

6th row: K3, *p3, k3; rep from * to end.

Rep 1st to 6th rows once more.

These 12 rows form the edging.

Cast off or cont as required.

Double Diamond Edging

Worked lengthways over 9 sts.

1st and every alt row (right side): Knit.

2nd row: K3, k2tog, yo, k2tog, [yo, k1] twice. (10 sts)

4th row: K2, [k2tog, yo] twice, k3, yo, k1. (11 sts)

6th row: K1, [k2tog, yo] twice, k5, yo, k1. (12 sts)

8th row: K3, [yo, k2tog] twice, k1, k2tog, yo, k2tog. (11 sts)

10th row: K4, yo, k2tog, yo, k3tog, yo, k2tog. (10 sts)

12th row: K5, yo, k3tog, yo, k2tog. (9 sts)

Rep these 12 rows.

Hunter's Rib

Worked from bottom edge upwards.

Starts and ends with multiple of 11 sts + 4 sts.

Note: cast on using the thumb method.

1st row (right side): P4, *[k1 tbl, p1] 3 times, k1 tbl, p4; rep from * to end.

2nd row: K4, *p1, [k1 tbl, p1] 3 times, k4; rep from * to end.

Rep 1st and 2nd rows 4 more times.

These 10 rows form the edging.

Cast off or cont as required.

Lace Cable

Worked from bottom edge upwards.

Starts and ends with multiple of 11 sts + 7 sts.

Note: cast on using the thumb method.

1st and every alt row: Purl.

2nd row (right side): K1, *yo, ssk, k1, k2tog, yo, k6; rep from *, ending last rep k1.

4th row: K2, *yo, sk2po, yo, k1, C6B, k1; rep from *, ending yo, sk2po, yo, k2.

6th row: As 2nd row.

8th row: K2, *yo, sk2po, yo, k8; rep from *, ending last last rep k2.

Rep 1st to 8th rows once more.

17th row: Purl.

These 17 rows form the edging.

Cast off or cont as required.

Points and Bobbles

Worked lengthways over 6 sts.

Special abbreviation: MB = make bobble. (K1, p1, k1, p1, k1) in next st, [turn, sl 1, k4] 4 times, turn, 1 at a time, lift 2nd, 3rd, 4th and 5th st over 1st st.

1st row (right side): K3, yo, k3. (7 sts)
2nd and every alt row: Knit.
3rd row: K3, yo, k4. (8 sts)
5th row: K3, yo, k5. (9 sts)
7th row: K3, yo, k6. (10 sts)
9th row: K3, yo, k7. (11 sts)
11th row: K3, yo, k7, MB. (12 sts)
12th row: Cast off 6 sts, k to end. (6 sts)
Rep these 12 rows.

Ribbed Tags

Worked from bottom edge upwards.

Starts and ends with multiple of 9 sts.

Note: cast on using the thumb method. Each tag is worked separately and then joined on one row.

Cast on 9 sts.

1st row (right side): Knit.

2nd row: K1, p to last st, k1.

3rd and 4th rows: As 2nd row.

5th and 6th rows: As 1st row.

Rep 1st to 5th rows once more.

1st to 11th rows form one tag. Cut yarn and leave finished tag on needle. On the free needle, cast on 9 sts and work 2nd tag.

Cont in this way until there are as many tags as required.

Join tags

Do not cut yarn after completing the last tag, but turn and knit across all tags on needle.

Rep 1st to 6th rows once more.

These 18 rows form the edging.

Cast off or cont as required.

Tassel Fringe

Worked lengthways over any odd number of sts.

1st row (right side): *K2tog, yo; rep from * to last st, k1.
Work 2 rows in garter stitch.
Cast off or cont as required.

Tassels

Cut two 10cm (4in) lengths of yarn for each eyelet. Fold
two strands in half together. Wrong side facing, put a
crochet hook through an eyelet and pull the folded loop
of the strands through. Slip the cut ends through the loop
and pull taut. When all the tassels have been added, trim
the ends of the strands.

Scalloped Eyelet Edging

Worked lengthways over 11 sts.

1st row (right side): Sl 1, k2, yo, p2tog, yo, skpo,
[yo, skpo] twice.
2nd row: Yo, *p1, (k1, p1) in next st; rep from *
twice more, p2, yo, p2tog, k1 tbl. (15 sts)
3rd row: Sl 1, k2, yo, p2tog, k10.
4th row: Sl 1, p11, yo, p2tog, k1 tbl.
5th row: Sl 1, k2, yo, p2tog, k10.
6th row: Cast off 4 sts purlwise, p7, yo, p2tog, k1 tbl.
(11 sts)
Rep these 6 rows.

Big Lace Check

Worked from bottom edge upwards.

Starts and ends with multiple of 18 sts + 9 sts.

Note: cast on using the thumb method.

1st and foll alt row (wrong side): Purl.

2nd row: K1, *[yo, k2tog] 4 times, k10; rep from * to last 8 sts, [yo, k2tog] 4 times.

4th row: *[Skpo, yo] 4 times, k10; rep from * to last 9 sts, [skpo, yo] 4 times, k1.

Rep 1st to 4th rows twice more.

13th and foll alt row: Purl.

14th row: *K10, [yo, k2tog] 4 times; rep from * to last 9 sts, k9.

16th row: K9 *[skpo, yo] 4 times, k10; rep from * to end.

Rep 13th to 16th rows twice more.

These 24 rows form the edging.

Cast off or cont as required.

Heart Appliqué

Cast on 2 sts.

1st row (right side): Inc, k1. (3 sts)

2nd and every alt row: Purl.

3rd row: K1, [M1, k1] twice. (5 sts)

5th row: K2, M1, k1, M1, k2. (7 sts)

7th row: K3, M1, k1, M1, k3. (9 sts)

9th row: K4, M1, k1, M1, k4. (11 sts)

11th row: K5, M1, k1, M1, k5. (13 sts)

13th row: K 6, k in back loop of st below next st then k in next st, k6. (14 sts)

15th row: Ssk, k3, k2tog, turn.

Cont on these 5 sts only and leave rem sts on a st holder.

17th row: Ssk, k1, k2tog. (3 sts)

18th row: P3tog tbl.

Fasten off.

Next row (right side): Rejoin yarn to inner end of rem sts, ssk, k3, k2tog. (5 sts)

Next right side row: Ssk, k1, k2tog. (3 sts)

Next row: P3tog.

Fasten off.

Lace Ruffle

Worked from bottom edge upwards.

Starts with twice the number of sts needed that is a multiple of 4 sts + 2 sts.

Ends with multiple of 2 sts + 1 st.

Note: cast on using the thumb method.

1st row (wrong side): Knit.

2nd row: K1, *skpo, yo2, k2tog; rep from *, ending k1.

3rd row: P1, *p1, (p1, k1) in yo2, p1; rep from *, ending p1.

Rep 2nd and 3rd rows 6 more times.

10th row: [K2tog] to end.

11th row: Purl.

12th row: K1, *yo, k2tog; rep from * to end.

Work 3 rows st st.

These 15 rows form the edging.

Cast off or cont as required.

Tiny Bobble Braid

Worked lengthways over 5 sts.

Special abbreviation: MB = make bobble. (K1, p1, k1, p1, k1) in next st, 1 at a time, lift 2nd, 3rd, 4th and 5th sts over 1st st.

1st and 2nd rows: Sl 1, k4.
3rd row (right side): Sl 1, k1, MB, k2.
4th row: Sl 1, k4.
Rep these 4 rows, ending with a 2nd row.

Eyelet Rib

Worked from bottom edge upwards.

Starts and ends with multiple of 8 sts + 2 sts.

Note: cast on using the thumb method.

1st row: *P2, k2; rep from *, ending p2.
2nd row: K2, p2, *yo, k2tog, p2; rep from *, ending k2.
Rep 1st and 2nd rows 3 more times.
9th row: P2, *k6, p2; rep from * to end.
10th row: K2, p6, *yo, k2tog, p6; rep from *, ending k2.
Rep 9th and 10th rows once more, then 9th row once more.
These 13 rows form the edging.
Cast off or cont as required.

Diagonal Rib and Scallop

Worked lengthways over 8 sts.

1st foundation row (right side): K6, inc, yf, sl 1 purlwise. (9 sts)

2nd foundation row: K1 tbl, k1, [yo, skpo, k1] twice, yf, sl 1 purlwise. (9 sts)

1st row: K1 tbl, k to last st, inc, turn and cast on 2 sts. (12 sts)

2nd row: K1, inc, k2, [yo, skpo, k1] twice, yo, k1, yf, sl 1 purlwise. (14 sts)

3rd row: K1 tbl, k to last 2 sts, inc, yf, sl 1 purlwise. (15 sts)

4th row: K1 tbl, inc, k2, [yo, skpo, k1] 3 times, k1, yf, sl 1 purlwise. (16 sts)

5th row: K1 tbl, k to last 2 sts, k2tog. (15 sts)

6th row: Sl 1 purlwise, k1, psso, skpo, k4, [yo, skpo, k1] twice, yf, sl 1 purlwise. (13 sts)

7th row: K1 tbl, k to last 2 sts, k2tog. (12 sts)

8th row: Cast off 3 sts, k2, yo, skpo, k1, yo, skpo, yf, sl 1 purlwise. (9 sts)

Rep these 8 rows.

Fern and Bobble Edging

Worked lengthways over 21 sts.

Special abbreviation: MB = make bobble. (K1, k1 tbl, k1) in next st, turn, k3, turn, p3, turn, k3, sk2po.

1st row (right side): K2, k2tog, yo2, [k2tog] twice, yo2, k2tog, k2, yo2, k2tog k7. (22 sts)

2nd row: K9, p1, k4, [p1, k3] twice.

3rd row: K2, k2tog, yo2, [k2tog] twice, yo2, k2tog, k1, MB, k2, yo2, k2tog, k6. (23 sts)

4th row: K8, p1, k6, [p1, k3] twice.

5th row: K2, k2tog, yo2, [k2tog] twice, yo2, k2tog, k3, MB, k2, yo2, k2tog, k5. (24 sts)

6th row: K7, p1, k8, [p1, k3] twice.

7th row: K2, k2tog, yo2, [k2tog] twice, yo2, k2tog, k5, MB, k2, yo2, k2tog, k4. (25 sts)

8th row: K6, p1, k10, [p1, k3] twice.

9th row: K2, k2tog, yo2, [k2tog] twice, yo2, k2tog, k7, MB, k2, yo2, k2tog, k3. (26 sts)

10th row: K5, p1, k12, [p1, k3] twice.

11th row: K2, k2tog, yo2, [k2tog] twice, yo2, k2tog, k9, MB, k2, yo2, k2tog, k2. (27 sts)

12th row: K4, p1, k14, [p1, k3] twice.

13th row: K2, k2tog, yo2, [k2tog] twice, yo2, k2tog, k11, MB, k2, yo2, k2tog, k1. (28 sts)

14th row: K3, p1, k16, [p1, k3] twice.

15th row: K2, k2tog, yo2, [k2tog] twice, yo2, k2tog, k18. (28 sts)

16th row: Cast off 7 sts, knit until there are 13 sts on RH needle, [p1, k3] twice. (21 sts)

Rep these 16 rows.

Garter Stitch Points

Worked from bottom edge upwards.

Ends with multiple of 13 sts.

Note: Each point is worked separately and then joined on one row.

Cast on 2 sts.

1st row: K2.

2nd row: Yo, k2. (3 sts)

3rd row: Yo, k3. (4 sts)

4th row: Yo, k4. (5 sts)

5th row: Yo, k5. (6 sts)

6th row: Yo, k6. (7 sts)

7th row: Yo, k7. (8 sts)

8th row: Yo, k8. (9 sts)

9th row: Yo, k9. (10 sts)

10th row: Yo, k10. (11 sts)

11th row: Yo, k11. (12 sts)

12th row: Yo, k12. (13 sts)

1st to 12th rows form one point. Cut yarn and leave finished point on needle. On the same needle, cast on 2 sts and work 2nd point.

Cont in this way until there are as many points as required.

Do not cut yarn after completing the last point, but turn and knit across all points on needle.

Work 9 rows in garter st.

These 21 rows form the edging.

Cast off or cont as required

Weave in loose ends.

Casing and Drawstring

Worked from bottom edge upwards or top edge downwards.

Starts and ends with multiple of 2 sts + 1 st.

Starting with a k row, work 7 rows st st.

8th row (wrong side): Knit.

Starting with a k row, work 3 rows st st.

12th row (drawstring opening): P to centre 3 sts, cast off 3 sts, p to end.

13th row: K to cast off sts, cast on 3 sts, k to end.

Starting with a p row, work 3 rows st st.

Fold hem over at ridge row.

17th row: *Slip horizontal strand from 1st cast-on st onto LH needle, then k this strand tog with first st on needle; rep from * to end.

Cont as required.

Cord

Make a twisted cord, a plaited cord or a 3-st I-cord of required length.

Thread cord through casing.

Double Pintuck

Worked from bottom edge upwards.

Starts and ends with multiple of 2 sts + 1 st.

Note: two colours of yarn, A and B, are used here, but the pintuck can be worked in one colour if preferred.

Starting with a k row and A, work 12 rows st st.

13th row (right side): *Lift horizontal strand from cast-on edge below st on needle and place on LH needle, then k this strand tog with st on needle; rep from * to end.

Work 7 rows st st.

Change to B and work 12 rows st st.

33rd row (right side): * Lift stitch loop from 12 rows below st on needle and place on LH needle, then k this loop tog with st on needle; rep from * to end.

These 33 rows form the edging.

Cast off or cont as required.

Moss Diamonds Edging

Worked from bottom edge upwards.

Starts and ends with multiple of 10 sts + 9 sts.

Note: cast on using the thumb method.

1st row (right side): P1, *k1, p1; rep from * to end.

2nd row: As 1st row.

3rd row: K4, *p1, k9; rep from * to last 5 sts, p1, k4.

4th row: P3, *k1, p1, k1, p7; rep from * to last 6 sts, k1, p1, k1, p3.

5th row: K2, *[p1, k1] twice, p1, k5; rep from * to last 7 sts, [p1, k1] twice, p1, k2.

6th row: [P1, k1] 4 times, *p3, [k1, p1] 3 times, k1; rep from * to last st, p1.

7th row: P1, *k1, p1; rep from * to end.

8th row: As 6th row.

9th row: As 5th row.

10th row: As 4th row.

11th row: As 3rd row.

12th row: As 2nd row.

13th row: As 1st row.

These 13 rows form the edging.

Cast off or cont as required.

Noughts and Crosses Trim

Worked over lengthways over 16 sts.

1st row (right side): Sl 1, k15.
2nd row: Sl 1, k1, p12, k2.
Rep 1st and 2nd rows once more.
5th row: Sl 1, k1, C6B, C6F, k2.
6th row: Sl 1, k1, p12, k2.
Rep 1st to 6th rows once more.
13th row: Sl 1, k15.
14th row: Sl 1, k1, p12, k2.
Rep 13th and 14th rows once more.
17th row: Sl 1, k1, C6F, C6B, k2.
18th row: Sl 1, k1, p12, k2.
Rep 13th to 18th rows once more.
Rep these 24 rows.

Beaded Cable Cast On

Worked from bottom edge upwards.
Starts and ends with multiple of 2 sts + 1 st.
Note: thread beads onto knitting yarn before casting on, 1 bead for every alt st, less 2, to give a selvedge st at each end.

Place a slip knot on the needle.
Cast on 1 st.
*Slide 1 bead up to sit behind the st, insert RH needle knitwise into st and draw loop through, drawing bead through with it. Sip loop onto LH needle and ensure bead is sitting at base of st.
Cast on 1 st.
Rep from * until 1 less than required number of sts are on LH needle.
Cast on 1 st.
This forms the edging.
Cont as required. Usually the 1st row will be a right side row to show the beads to best effect.

Ric-rac

Worked from bottom edge upwards.

Starts with multiple of 10 sts + 1 st.

Ends with multiple of 8 sts + 1 st before casting off.

Note: cast on using the thumb method.

1st row (right side): K4, *sk2po, k7; rep from *, ending sk2po, k4.

2nd and foll alt row: Knit.

3rd row: K1, *M1, k2, sk2po, k2, M1, k1; rep from * to end.

5th row: As 3rd row.

6th row: Knit.

Cast off, working k1, *M1, k7, M1, k1; rep from * across row.

These 6 rows form the edging.

Scallop Edging

Worked from top edge downwards.

Starts and ends with multiple of 13 sts + 2 sts.

Note: cast on using the thumb method.

1st row (right side): K1, *skpo, k9, k2tog; rep from * to last st, k1.

2nd and foll alt row: Purl.

3rd row: K1, *skpo, k7, k2tog; rep from * to last st, k1.

5th row: K1, *skpo, yo, [k1, yo] 5 times, k2tog; rep from * to last st, k1.

6th row: Knit.

These 6 rows form the edging.

Cast off.

Lace Picot

Worked from bottom edge upwards.

Starts and ends with multiple of 8 sts + 1 st.

Note: cast on using the thumb method.

Starting with a k row, work 3 rows st st.

4th row (wrong side): P1, *yo, p2tog; rep from * to end.

Work 4 rows st st.

9th row: K2 *yo, k2tog; rep from *, ending k1.

Work 3 rows st st.

13th row: K1, *yo, ssk, k3, k2tog, yo, k1; rep from * to end.

14th row: P2, yo, p2tog, k1, p2tog tbl, yo, *p3, yo, p2tog, p1, p2tog tbl, yo; rep from *, ending p2.

15th row: K2, *k1, yo, k3tog, yo, k4; rep from *, ending last rep k3.

16th row: P2, p2tog tbl, yo, p1, yo, p2tog, *p3, p2tog tbl, yo, p1, yo, p2tog; rep from *, ending p2.

17th row: K1, k2tog, *yo, k3, yo, ssk, k1, k2tog; rep from *, ending last rep yo, k3, yo, ssk, k1.

18th row: P2tog tbl, yo, p5, *yo, p3tog, yo, p5; rep from *, ending yo, p2tog.

Work 2 rows st st.

21st row: As 9th row.

Work 3 rows st st.

Fold hem to back along row 4 and slip stitch in place.

These 24 rows form the edging.

Cast off or cont as required.

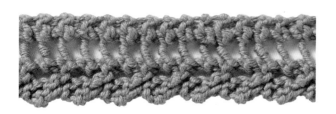

Bird's Eye Edging

Worked lengthways over 7 sts.

1st row (right side): K1, k2tog, yo2, k2tog, yo2, k2. (9 sts)
2nd row: K3, [p1, k2] twice.
3rd row: K1, k2tog, yo2, k2tog, k4.
4th row: Cast off 2 sts, k3, p1, k2. (7 sts)
Rep these 4 rows.

Twisted Fringe

Worked lengthways over 3 sts.

Work 3 rows in garter stitch.
4th row (wrong side): Cast on 10 sts, inc in each of these 10 sts, casting off one st as each st is made, k2. (3 sts)
Rep these 4 rows, ending with a 2nd row.

Cherry Basket

Worked from bottom edge upwards.

Starts and ends with multiple of 11 sts + 2 sts.

Note: cast on using the thumb method.

Special abbreviation: MB = make bobble. (K1, p1, k1, p1, k1) in next st, turn, p5, turn, 1 at a time, lift 2nd, 3rd, 4th and 5th sts over 1st st. (K next st tbl).

Work 3 rows in garter stitch.

4th and every alt row: Purl.

5th row (right side): *K5, k2tog, yo, k4; rep from *, ending k2.

7th row: *K4, k2tog, yo, k1, yo, ssk, k2; rep from *, ending k2.

9th row: *K3, [k2tog, yo] twice, k1, yo, ssk, k1; rep from *, ending k2.

11th row: *K2, [k2tog, yo] twice, k1, [yo, ssk] twice; rep from *, ending k2.

13th row: *K3, k2tog, yo, k1, MB, k1, yo, ssk, k1; rep from *, ending k2.

15th row: *K4, MB, k3, MB, k2; rep from *, ending k2.

17th row: *K6, MB, k4; rep from *, ending k2.

19th row: Knit.

20th row: Purl.

Work 4 rows in garter stitch.

These 24 rows form the edging.

Cast off or cont as required.

Wheatsheaf Cable Rib

Worked from bottom edge upwards.

Starts and ends with multiple of 16 sts + 8 sts.

Note: cast on using the thumb method.

1st, 3rd and 5th rows (right side): P1, k6, *p4, k2, p4, k6; rep from *, ending p1.

2nd and 4th rows: K11, p2, *k14, p2; rep from *, ending k11.

6th row: K1, p6, *k4, p2, k4, p6; rep from *, ending k1.

7th row: P3, k2, *T4F, p2, k2, p2, T4B, k2; rep from *, ending p3.

8th row: K3, p2, *k2, p2; rep from *, ending k3.

9th row: P3, k2, *p2, T4F, k2, T4B, p2, k2; rep from *, ending p3.

10th row: K3, p2, *k4, p6, k4, p2; rep from *, ending k3.

11th, 13th and 15th rows: P3, k2, *p4, k6, p4, k2; rep from *, ending p3.

12th and 14th rows: K3, p2, *k14, p2; rep from *, ending k3.

16th and 18th rows: As 10th row.

17th row: P3, k2, *p4, C6B, p4, k2; rep from *, ending p3.

19th, 21st and 23rd rows: As 11th row.

20th and 22nd rows: As 12th row.

24th row: As 10th row.

25th row: P3, k2, *p2, T4B, k2, T4F, p2, k2; rep from *, ending p3.

26th row: As 8th row.

27th row: P3, k2, *T4B, p2, k2, p2, T4F, k2; rep from *, ending p3.

28th row: As 6th row.

29th row: As 1st row.

30th row: As 2nd row.

These 30 rows form the edging.

Cast off or cont as required.

Beaded Garter Edging

Worked lengthways over 4 sts.

Note: Thread beads onto knitting yarn before casting on, 1 bead for each 3rd row.

1st row (right side): Sl 1, k3.

2nd row: As 1st row.

3rd row: Slide a bead up to needle, wyf insert RH needle tbl in first 2 sts, yo, k2tog tbl, k2.

4th row: Sl 1, k3.

Rep these 4 rows.

Little Bobble Rib

Worked from bottom edge upwards.

Starts and ends with multiple of 8 sts + 3 sts.

Special abbreviation: MB = make bobble. (P1, k1, p1, k1) in next st, then, 1 at a time, lift 2nd, 3rd and 4th sts over 1st st.

Note: cast on using the thumb method.

1st row (right side): K3, *p2, MB, p2, k3; rep from * to end.

2nd row: P3, *k5, p3; rep from * to end.

3rd row: K3, *p5, k3; rep from * to end.

4th row: As 2nd row.

Rep these 4 rows once more then rep 1st row once more.

These 9 rows form the edging.

Cast off or cont as required.

Diamond Edge

Worked lengthways over 12 sts.

1st and every alt row (right side): K1, yo, p2tog, k to end.

2nd row: K2, yo, k3, yo, skpo, k2, yo, p2tog, k1. (13 sts)

4th row: K2, yo, k5, yo, skpo, k1, yo, p2tog, k1. (14 sts)

6th row: K2, yo, k3, yo, skpo, k2, yo, skpo, yo, p2tog, k1.
(15 sts)

8th row: K1, k2tog, yo, skpo, k3, k2tog, yo, k2, yo, p2tog, k1.
(14 sts)

10th row: K1, k2tog, yo, skpo, k1, k2tog, yo, k3, yo, p2tog,
k1. (13 sts)

12th row: K1, k2tog, yo, sk2po, yo, k4, yo, p2tog, k1.
(12 sts)

Rep these 12 rows.

Leaf Braid

Worked lengthways over 17 sts.

1st row (right side): Sl 1, k3, [k2tog, yo] twice, k1, [yo, skpo] twice, k4.

2nd row: Sl 1, k5, p5, k6.

3rd row: Sl 1, k2, k2tog, yo, k2tog, k1, [yo, k1] twice, skpo, yo, skpo, k3.

4th row: Sl 1, k4, p7, k5.

5th row: Sl 1, k1, k2tog, yo, k2tog, k2, yo, k1, yo, k2, skpo, yo, skpo, k2.

6th row: Sl 1, k3, p9, k4.

7th row: Sl 1, k2tog, yo, k2tog, k3, yo, k1, yo, k3, skpo, yo, skpo, k1.

8th row: Sl 1, k2, p11, k3.

9th row: Sl 1, k2, yo, skpo, k7, k2tog, yo, k3.

10th row: Sl 1, k3, p9, k4.

11th row: Sl 1, k3, yo, skpo, k5, k2tog, yo, k4.

12th row: Sl 1, k4, p7, k5.

13th row: Sl 1, k4, yo, skpo, k3, k2tog, yo, k5.

14th row: Sl 1, k5, p5, k6.

15th row: Sl 1, k5, yo, skpo, k1, k2tog, yo, k6.

16th row: Sl 1, k6, p3, k7.

17th row: Sl 1, k6, yo, sk2po, yo, k7.

18th row: Sl 1, k7, p1, k8.

Rep these 18 rows.

Openwork Picot

Worked lengthways over 3 sts.

Cast on 3 sts.
*Cast off 2 sts. (1 st)
Slip this st onto LH needle.
Cast on 2 sts. (3 sts)
Rep from * for required length.
Cast off 2 sts. (1 st)
Without turning, work along straight edge of picot: **yo, put tip of LH needle under bar across top of picot and knit into this bar; rep from ** to end.
Work 2 rows in garter stitch.
This cast on and 2 rows form the edging.
Cast off or cont as required.

Beaded Cord

Worked lengthways over 5 sts on double-pointed needles.
Note: Thread beads onto knitting yarn before casting on, 1 bead for every 3rd row.

1st and 2nd rows: Knit, do not turn, slide sts to other end of needle.
3rd row: K2, PB, k2, do not turn, slide sts to other end of needle.
Rep these 3 rows.

Lacy Arrow Edging

Worked lengthways over 21 sts.

1st row (right side): K3, yo, k2tog, p2, yo, skpo, k3, k2tog, yo, p2, k1, yo, k2tog, k2.

2nd and every alt row: K3, yo, k2tog tbl, k2, p7, k3, yo, k2tog tbl, k2.

3rd row: K3, yo, k2tog, p2, k1, yo, skpo, k1, k2tog, yo, k1, p2, k1, yo, k2tog, k2.

5th row: K3, yo, k2tog, p2, k2, yo, sk2po, yo, k2, p2, k1, yo, k2tog, k2.

6th row: As 2nd row.

Rep these 6 rows.

Catherine Wheels Braid

Worked lengthways over 19 sts.

Special abbreviation: work 5tog = work 5 sts together. Skpo, k3tog, pass the st resulting from skpo over the st resulting from k3tog.

1st and every alt row (wrong side): Sl 1, k2, p to last 3 sts, k3.

2nd row: Sl 1, k7, sl 3, yf, pass same slipped sts back to left-hand needle, yb, knit 3 slipped sts, k8.

4th row: Sl 1, k5, k3tog, yo, inc2, yo, k3tog tbl, k6.

6th row: Sl 1, k3, k3tog, yo, k2tog, yo, inc2, yo, skpo, yo, k3tog tbl, k4.

8th row: Sl 1, k2, [k2tog, yo] 3 times, k1 tbl, [yo, skpo] 3 times, k3.

10th row: Sl 1, k3, [yo, k2tog] twice, yo, sk2po, [yo, skpo] twice, yo, k4.

12th row: Sl 1, k2, [skpo, yo] 3 times, k1 tbl, [yo, k2tog] 3 times, k3.

14th row: Sl 1, k3, inc, yo, skpo, yo, work 5tog, yo, k2tog, yo, inc, k4.

16th row: Sl 1, k5, inc, yo, work 5tog, yo, inc, k6.

Rep these 16 rows.

Ornamental Diamond Edging

Worked lengthways over 17 sts.

1st foundation row (right side): K1, yo, skpo, k1, k2tog, yo, k7, yo, k2tog, k2.

2nd foundation row: P3, yo, p2tog, p12.

1st row: K1, yo, k2tog, yo, k3, yo, skpo, k5, yo, k2tog, k2. (18 sts)

2nd row: P3, yo, p2tog, p13.

3rd row: K1, yo, k2tog, yo, k5, yo, skpo, k4, yo, k2tog, k2. (19 sts)

4th row: P3, yo, p2tog, p14.

5th row: K1, yo, k2tog, yo, k3, yo, skpo, k2, yo, skpo, k3, yo, k2tog, k2. (20 sts)

6th row: P3, yo, p2tog, p15.

7th row: K1, yo, k2tog, yo, k3, [yo, skpo] twice, k2, yo, skpo, k2, yo, k2tog, k2. (21 sts)

8th row: P3, yo, p2tog, p16.

9th row: K1, yo, k2tog, yo, k3, [yo, skpo] 3 times, k2, yo, skpo, k1, yo, k2tog, k2. (22 sts)

10th row: P3, yo, p2tog, p17.

11th row: Skpo, [yo, skpo] twice, k2, [yo, skpo] twice, k1, k2tog, yo, k3, yo, k2tog, k2. (21 sts)

12th row: P3, yo, p2tog, p16.

13th row: Skpo, [yo, skpo] twice, k2, yo, skpo, k1, k2tog, yo, k4, yo, k2tog, k2. (20 sts)

14th row: P3, yo, p2tog, p15.

15th row: Skpo, [yo, skpo] twice, k3, k2tog, yo, k5, yo, k2tog, k2. (19 sts)

16th row: P3, yo, p2tog, p14.

17th row: Skpo, [yo, skpo] twice, k1, k2tog, yo, k6, yo, k2tog, k2. (18 sts)

18th row: P3, yo, p2tog, p13.

19th row: Skpo, yo, skpo, k1, k2tog, yo, k7, yo, k2tog, k2. (17 sts)

20th row: P3, yo, p2tog, p12.

Rep the 1st to 20th rows.

Beaded Loop Rib

Worked from bottom edge upwards.

Starts and ends with multiple of 2 sts + 1 st.

Note: thread beads onto knitting yarn before casting on, 5 beads for each loop.

1st row (right side): [K1, p1] to last st, k1.

2nd and foll alt row: [P1, k1] to last st, p1.

3rd row: K1, p1, *k1, yf, slide 5 beads up to RH needle, p1 tbl, k1, p1; rep from * to last st, k1.

5th row: *K1, yf, slide 5 beads to the base of the RH needle, p1 tbl, k1, p1; rep from * to last st, k1.

6th row: As 2nd row.

These 6 rows form the edging.

Cast off or cont as required.

Picot Point Cast Off

Worked from upper edge downwards.

Multiple of 3 sts + 2 sts.

Note: cast on using the cable method.

Cast off 2 sts, *slip rem st on RH needle onto LH needle, cast on 2 sts, cast off 4 sts; rep from * to end and fasten off rem st.

Cabled Fringe

Worked lengthways over 14 sts.

Note: two colours of yarn, A and B, are used, but the edging can be worked in one colour if preferred.

Using cable method, cast on 9 sts with A and 5 sts with B.

1st and 5th rows (right side): K5 B, k9 A.

2nd and every alt row: P9 A, p5 B.

3rd row: K5 B, with A, C6F, k3.

7th row: K5 B, with A, k3, C6B.

8th row: As 2nd row.

Rep 1st to 8th rows as required, ending with a 2nd row.

Next row: K4 B, cast off rem sts.

Slip 4 sts off needle and unravel across knitted fabric to create fringe. Loops can be cut to make strands.

Star Braid

Worked lengthways over 17 sts.

1st row (wrong side): Sl 1, k1, p13, k2.
2nd row: Sl 1, k16.
3rd row: Sl 1, k1, p6, k1, p6, k2.
4th row: Sl 1, k16.
5th row: Sl 1, k2, [p5, k1] twice, k2.
6th row: Sl 1, k2, p1, k9, p1, k3.
7th row: Sl 1, k1, p2, [k1, p3] twice, k1, p2, k2.
8th row: Sl 1, k4, p1, k5, p1, k5.
9th row: Sl 1, k1, p4, [k1, p1] twice, k1, p4, k2.

10th row: Sl 1, k6, p1, k1, p1, k7.
Rep 10th row twice more.
13th row: Sl 1, k1, p4, [k1, p1] twice, k1, p4, k2.
14th row: Sl 1, k4, p1, k5, p1, k5.
15th row: Sl 1, k1, p2, [k1, p3] twice, k1, p2, k2.
16th row: Sl 1, k2, p1, k9, p1, k3.
17th row: Sl 1, k2, [p5, k1] twice, k2.
18th row: Sl 1, k16.
19th row: Sl 1, k1, p6, k1, p6, k2.
20th row: Sl 1, k16.
Rep 3rd to 20th rows.

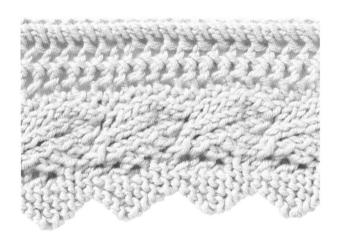

Fancy Leaf Edging

Worked lengthways over 17 sts.

1st row (right side): K3, yo, p2tog, yo, p2tog, yo, k1 tbl, k2tog, p1, yb, skpo, k1 tbl, yo, k3.

2nd row: K3, p3, k1, p3, k2, yo, p2tog, yo, p2tog, k1.

Rep 1st and 2nd rows once more.

5th row: K3, yo, p2tog, yo, p2tog, yo, k1 tbl, yo, k2tog, p1, yb, skpo, yo, k4. (18 sts)

6th row: K4, p2, k1, p4, k2, yo, p2tog, yo, p2tog, k1.

7th row: K3, yo, p2tog, yo, p2tog, yo, k1 tbl, k1, k1 tbl, yo, sk2po, yo, k5. (19 sts)

8th row: K5, p7, k2, yo, p2tog, yo, p2tog, k1.

9th row: K3, yo, p2tog, yo, p2tog, yo, k1 tbl, k3, k1 tbl, yo, k7. (21 sts)

10th row: Cast off 4 sts knitwise, k2, p7, k2, yo, p2tog, yo, p2tog, k1. (17 sts)

Rep these 10 rows.

Unravelled Fringe With Eyelets

Worked lengthways over any number of sts.

1st row (right side): K5, k2tog, yo, k to end.
2nd row: Purl.
Rep 1st and 2nd rows as required, ending with a 2nd row.
Next row: K5, cast off rem sts.
Slip 5 sts off needle and unravel across knitted fabric to create fringe.

Double Picots and Eyelets

Worked from bottom edge upwards.
Worked over any odd number of sts.
Note: Use cable cast on throughout.

Cast on 6 sts, cast off 4 sts, slip st on RH needle onto LH needle, cast on 4 sts, cast off 4 sts, slip st on RH needle onto LH needle, *cast on 5 sts, cast off 4 sts, slip st on RH needle onto LH needle, cast on 4 sts, cast off 4 sts, slip st on RH needle onto LH needle; rep from * until a single picot less than the required number of sts has been made.
1st row (right side): *K1, yo; rep from * to last st, k1.
This cast on and row form the edging.
Cast off or cont as required.

Garter Bunting

Worked lengthways over 8 sts.

1st row (right side): Sl 1, k7.

2nd row: Ssk, k6. (7 sts)

3rd row: Sl 1, k6.

4th row: Ssk, k5. (6 sts)

5th row: Sl 1, k5.

6th row: Ssk, k4. (5 sts)

7th row: Sl 1, k4.

8th row: Ssk, k3. (4 sts)

9th row: Sl 1, k3.

10th row: Cast on 4 sts, k all 8 sts.

Rep these 10 rows, ending with a 9th row.

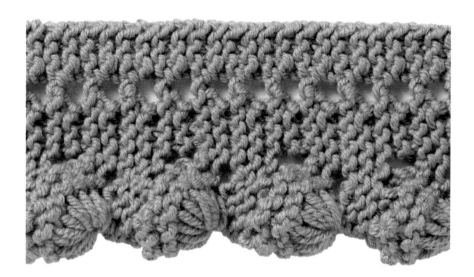

Puff Ball Cluster Edging

Worked lengthways over 13 sts.

1st row (wrong side): K2, k2tog, yo2, k2tog, k7.
2nd row: K9, p1, k3.
Work 2 rows in garter stitch.
5th row: K2, k2tog, yo2, k2tog, k2, [yo2, k1] 3 times, yo2, k2. (21 sts)
6th row: K3, [p1, k2] 3 times, p1, k4, p1, k3.
Work 2 rows in garter stitch.

9th row: K2, k2tog, yo2, k2tog, k15.
10th row: K12 wrapping yarn twice round needle for each st, yo2, k5, p1, k3. (23 sts)
11th row: K10, (p1, k1) in next st, slip next 12 sts to RH needle dropping extra loops., return sts to LH needle then k12tog. (13 sts)
12th row: Knit.
Rep these 12 rows.

Knitted Tassel

Special abbreviation: MT = make tail. Cast on 4 sts, cast off 4 sts.

Note: two colours of yarn are used, A and B. Cast on using the cable method throughout.

Head cover

Using A, cast on 6 sts.

1st row (wrong side): Purl.

2nd row: [K1, M1] to last st, k1. (11 sts)

3rd row: Purl.

4th row: [K1, M1] to last st, k1. (21 sts)

Join in B.

Starting with a p row, work 7 rows st st, changing colour every 2 rows, ending with 1 row in A. Cut B.

12th row: [K2tog] to last st, k1. (11 sts)

13th row: Purl.

14th row: [K2tog] to last st, k1. (6 sts)

15th row: [MT] to end.

Tail cast off row: *Cast on 19 sts, cast off 20 sts, slip st on RH needle back onto LH needle; rep from * to end.

Tassel

Wind yarn around a piece of card the required length of the tassel. Make a twisted cord and tie the ends around the top of the wound yarn so that the knot sits on top of the tassel. Bind off the head of the tassel.

Using mattress stitch and taking a 1 st seam, join half the seam on the head cover, stitching down from the cast on edge. Slip the cover over the head of the tassel, then join the rest of the seam. Stitch through the tassel at the base of the head to anchor the cover to the tassel.

Square Filet Edging

Worked lengthways over 15 sts.

Foundation row: Knit.

1st row (right side): K1, k2tog, yo2, k2tog, k1, yo2, k7, yo2, k2. (19 sts)

2nd row: K3, p1, k8, p1, k3, p1, k2.

3rd row: K1, k2tog, yo2, k2tog, k1, [yo2, k2tog] twice, k3, k2tog, yo2, k4. (22 sts)

4th row: K5, p1, k6, p1, k2, p1, k3, p1, k2.

5th row: K1, k2tog, yo2, k2tog, k1, yo2, [k2tog, k1, k2tog, yo2] twice, k6. (24 sts)

6th row: K7, [p1, k4] twice, p1, k3, p1, k2.

7th row: K1, k2tog, yo2, k2tog, k1, yo2, k2tog, k3, k2tog, yo2, k3tog, yo2, k8. (26 sts)

8th row: K9, p1, k2, p1, k6, p1, k3, p1, k2.

9th row: K1, k2tog, yo2, k2tog, k21.

10th row: Cast off 10 sts, k8, k2tog, k2, p1, k2. (15 sts)

Rep 1st to 10th rows.

Lacy Point Ruffle

Worked from bottom edge upwards.

Starts with twice the number of sts needed that is a multiple of 14 sts + 1 st.

Ends with multiple of 7 sts + 1 st.

Note: cast on using the thumb method.

1st row: Purl.

2nd row (right side): K1, *yo, k3, skpo, yo, sk2po, yo, k2tog, k3, yo, k1; rep from * to end.

Rep 1st and 2nd rows 5 more times, then rep 1st row once more.

14th row: *[Skpo] 4 times, [k2tog] 3 times; rep from * to last st, k1.

15th row: Purl.

16th row: K1, *yo, k2tog; rep from *, ending k1 if needed.

17th row: Purl.

18th row: Knit.

These 18 rows form the edging.

Cast off or cont as required.

Flower Bud Trim

Worked lengthways over 7 sts.

1st row (right side): K1 tbl, [p2, k1 tbl] twice.

2nd row: P1, [k2, p1 tbl] twice.

3rd row: K1 tbl, p2, (k1, p1, k1, p1, k1) in next st, p2, k1 tbl. (11 sts)

4th row: P1, k2, p5, k2, p1 tbl.

5th row: K1 tbl, p2, k5, p2, k1 tbl.

6th row: As 4th row.

7th row: K1 tbl, p2, skpo, k1, k2tog, p2, k1 tbl. (9 sts)

8th row: P1, k2, p3, k2, p1 tbl.

9th row: K1 tbl, p2, sk2po, p2, k1 tbl. (7 sts)

10th row: As 2nd row.

Rep these 10 rows, ending with a 1st row.

Picot Point Chain

Worked lengthways over 5 sts.

Note: cast on using the cable method.

*Cast off 4 sts, slip st on RH needle onto LH needle, cast on 4 sts; rep from * until chain is required length.

Ribbed Rib

Worked lengthways over 17 sts.

1st, 3rd, and 5th rows (right side): K5, [p2, k4] twice.

2nd and foll 2 alt rows: [P4, k2] twice, p5.

7th row: K1, [p4, k2] twice, p4.

8th row: [K4, p2] twice, k4, p1.

9th and 10th rows: As 1st and 2nd rows.

Rep these 10 rows, ending with a 4th row.

Star Flower Appliqué

Put a slip knot on the needle.

1st row (right side): (K1, k1 tbl, k1) in st. (3 sts)

2nd and every alt row: Purl.

3rd row: K1, [M1, k1] twice. (5 sts)

5th row: K1, M1, k3, M1, k1. (7 sts)

7th row: K1, M1, k5, M1, k1. (9 sts)

9th row: K1, M1, k7, M1, k1. (11 sts)

11th row: K1 tbl, k2tog, k5, ssk, k1. (9 sts)

13th row: K1 tbl, k2tog, k3, ssk, k1. (7 sts)

15th row: K1 tbl, k2tog, k1, ssk, k1. (5 sts)

17th row: K1 tbl, sk2po, k1. (3 sts)

19th row: Sk2po. (1 st)

Fasten off.

Make 4 more petals.

Press.

With slip knots in the centre and taking 1 st from each edge into seam, join the five petals from 1st to 10th rows.

Simple Ruffle

Worked from bottom edge upwards.

Starts with twice the number of sts needed.

Note: cast on using the thumb method. If an odd number of sts are required, delete 1 st from the final count, cast on double that number of sts + 1 st and on the decrease row, end k1.

1st row: Knit.

2nd row: Purl.

Rep 1st and 2nd rows as required, ending with a 2nd row.

Next row: [K2tog] to end.

These rows form the edging.

Cast off or cont as required.

Crown Edging

Worked from upper edge downwards.

Multiple of 5 sts.

Note: if working this as a separate edge to be sewn on, cast on using the cable method.

1st row (wrong side): Knit.

2nd row: Cast off 2 sts, * slip st on RH needle onto LH needle, [cast on 2 sts, cast off 2 sts, slip st onto LH needle] 3 times, cast on 2 sts, cast off 6 sts; rep from * to end and fasten off rem st.

These 2 rows form the edging.

Tassel Rib

Worked from bottom edge upwards.

Starts and ends with multiple of 6 sts + 1 st.

Note: cast on using the thumb method.

1st row (right side): *K4, p2; rep from *, ending k1.

2nd row: P1, *k2, p4; rep from * to end.

Rep 1st and 2nd rows 3 more times.

9th row: *Place RH needle between 4th and 5th st from tip of LH needle and draw through a loop, k this loop tog with next st, p2, k3; rep from *, ending k1.

These 9 rows form the edging.

Cast off or cont as required.

Layered Rib

Worked from bottom edge upwards.

Starts and ends with multiple of 2 sts + 1 st.

Note: two colours of yarn are used, A and B. Cast on same number of sts for each layer using the thumb method and A.

Bottom layer

1st row (right side): K1, *p1, k1; rep from * to end.

2nd row: P1, *k1, p1; rep from * to end.

Rep 1st row once more.

Change to B.

Rep 2nd and 1st rows four more times.

Place sts on spare needle.

Top layer

1st row (right side): K1, *p1, k1; rep from * to end.

Change to B.

2nd row: P1, *k1, p1; rep from * to end.

Using B, rep 1st and 2nd rows once more, then rep 1st row once more.

Wrong side facing, hold top layer in front of bottom layer. Using 3rd needle, work 1 st from each needle tog across row, working p1 *k1, p1; rep from * to end.

Rep 1st and 2nd rows once more.

These rows form the edging.

Cast off or cont as required.

Garter Scallops

Worked lengthways over 7 sts.

Foundation row: Knit.

1st row: K4, inc, k2. (8 sts)

2nd row: K1, inc, k6. (9 sts)

3rd row: K6, inc, k2. (10 sts)

4th row: K1, inc, k8. (11 sts)

5th row: K8, inc, k2. (12 sts)

6th row: K1, inc, k10. (13 sts)

7th row: K10, inc, k2. (14 sts)

8th row: K1, inc, k12. (15 sts)

9th row: K12, k2tog, k1. (14 sts)

10th row: K1, k2tog tbl, k11. (13 sts)

11th row: K10, k2tog, k1. (12 sts)

12th row: K1, k2tog tbl, k9 (11 sts)

13th row: K8, k2tog, k1. (10 sts)

14th row: K1, k2tog tbl, k7. (9 sts)

15th row: K6, k2tog, k1. (8 sts)

16th row: K1, k2tog tbl, k5. (7 sts)

Rep the 1st to 16th rows.

Scallops Trim

Worked from bottom edge upwards.

Starts with multiple of 12 sts.

Ends with multiple of 8 sts.

Note: cast on using the thumb method.

1st row (right side): Knit.

2nd row: Purl.

3rd row: *[K2tog] twice, [M1, k1] 4 times, [skpo] twice; rep from * to end.

4th row: Purl.

5th row: *[K2tog] twice, k4, [skpo] twice; rep from * to end.

Work 2 rows in garter stitch.

These 7 rows form the edging.

Cast off or cont as required.

Lacy Leaf Edging

Worked lengthways over 13 sts.

1st row (right side): K1, sk2po, yo, k5, yo, k1 tbl, yo, skpo, k1.

2nd and every alt row: Purl.

3rd row: K1, k1 tbl, yo, k1, k2tog tbl, p1, yb, skpo, k1, yo, k1 tbl, yo, skpo, k1.

5th row: As 3rd row.

7th row: K1, skpo, yo, k2tog tbl, p1, yb, skpo, [yo, k1 tbl] twice, yo, skpo, k1.

9th row: K1, skpo, yo, k3tog tbl, yo, k3, yo, k1 tbl, yo, skpo, k1.

10th row: Purl.

Rep these 10 rows.

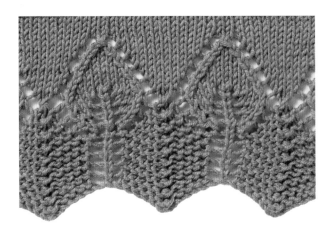

Leaf and Garter

Worked from bottom edge upwards.

Starts and ends with multiple of 14 sts + 1 st.

Note: cast on using the thumb method.

1st row (right side): K1, yo, p5, p3tog, *p5, yo, k1, yo, p5, p3tog; rep from *, ending p5, yo, k1.

2nd and every alt row: Purl.

Rep 1st and 2nd rows 5 more times.

13th row: K1, yo, skpo, yo, p3, p3tog, *p3, yo, k2tog, yo, k1, yo, skpo, yo, p3, p3tog; rep from *, ending p3, yo, k2tog, yo, k1.

15th row: K1, yo, k1, skpo, yo, p2, p3tog, *p2, yo, k2tog, [k1, yo] twice, k1, skpo, yo, p2, p3tog; rep from *, ending p2, yo, k2tog, k1, yo, k1.

17th row: K1, yo, k2, skpo, yo, p1, p3tog, *p1, yo, k2tog, k2, yo, k1, yo, k2, skpo, yo, p1, p3tog; rep from *, ending p1, yo, k2tog, k2, yo, k1.

19th row: K1, yo, k3, skpo, yo, p3tog, *yo, k2tog, k3, yo, k1, yo, k3, skpo, yo, p3tog; rep from *, ending yo, k2tog, k3, yo, k1.

21st row: K4, k2tog, yo, k2, *k1, yo, skpo, k7, k2tog, yo, k2; rep from *, ending k1, yo, skpo, k4.

23rd row: K3, k2tog, yo, k3, *k2, yo, skpo, k5, k2tog, yo, k3; rep from *, ending k2, yo, skpo, k3.

25th row: K2, k2tog, yo, k4, *k3, yo, skpo, k3, k2tog, yo, k4; rep from *, ending k3, yo, skpo, k2.

27th row: K1, k2tog, yo, k5, *k4, yo, skpo, k1, k2tog, yo, k5; rep from *, ending k4, yo, skpo, k1.

29th row: K2tog, yo, k6, *k5, yo, sk2po, yo, k6; rep from *, ending k5, yo, skpo.

30th row: Purl.

These 30 rows form the edging.

Cast off or cont as required.

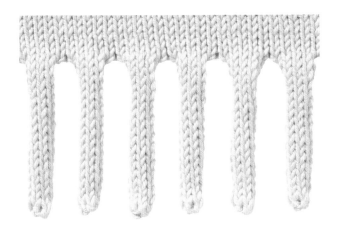

Cord Fringe

Worked from bottom edge upwards.

Starts and ends with multiple of 5 sts.

Cast on 5 sts onto double-pointed needles.

1st row: Knit, do not turn, slide sts to other end of needle.

Rep 1st row 16 more times.

Cut yarn and leave cord on spare straight needle.

Cast on 5 sts and work second cord. Cont in this way until there are as many cords as required.

Join cords

Do not cut yarn after completing the last cord, but turn and purl across all cords on straight needle.

These rows form the edging.

Cast off or cont as required.

Ridged Eyelet Border

Worked from bottom edge upwards.

Starts and ends with multiple of 2 sts + 1 st.

Note: cast on using the thumb method.

Work 3 rows in garter stitch.

4th row (wrong side): *P2tog, yo; rep from * to last st, p1.

Work 3 rows in garter stitch.

These 7 rows form the edging.

Cast off or cont as required.

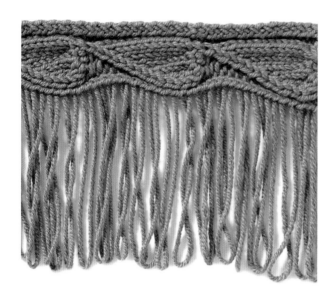

Leaf and Fringe

Worked lengthways over 13 sts.

Foundation row: [K5, p1] twice, k1.

1st row (right side): P1, k1 tbl, p2, ([k1, k1 tbl, yo] twice, k1, k1 tbl) in same st, p2, k1 tbl, k5. (20 sts)

2nd row: K5, p1 tbl, k2, p8, k2, p1 tbl, k1.

3rd row: P1, k1 tbl, p2, k6, k2tog, p2, k1 tbl, k5. (19 sts)

4th row: K5, p1 tbl, k2, p7, k2, p1 tbl, k1.

5th row: P1, k1 tbl, p2, k5, k2tog, p2, k1 tbl, k5. (18 sts)

6th row: K5, p1 tbl, k2, p6, k2, p1 tbl, k1.

7th row: P1, k1 tbl, p2, k4, k2tog, p2, k1 tbl, k5. (17 sts)

8th row: K5, p1 tbl, k2, p5, k2, p1 tbl, k1.

9th row: P1, k1 tbl, p2, k3, k2tog, p2, k1 tbl, k5. (16 sts)

10th row: K5, p1 tbl, k2, p4, k2, p1 tbl, k1.

11th row: P1, k1 tbl, p2, k2, k2tog, p2, k1 tbl, k5. (15 sts)

12th row: K5, p1 tbl, k2, p3, k2, p1 tbl, k1.

13th row: P1, k1 tbl, p2, k1, k2tog, p2, k1 tbl, k5. (14 sts)

14th row: K5, p1 tbl, k2, p2, k2, p1 tbl, k1.

15th row: P1, k1 tbl, p2, k2tog, p2, k1 tbl, k5. (13 sts)

16th row: K5, p1 tbl, k2, p1, k2, p1 tbl, k1.

Rep 1st to 16th rows as required, ending with a 16th row.

Next row: K5, cast off rem sts.

Slip 5 sts off needle and unravel across knitted fabric to create fringe. Loops can be cut to make strands.

Lace Stripes

Worked lengthways over 15 sts.

Note: to prevent holes forming when turning, wrap the yarn around the next stitch in this way: turn, leaving the yarn at the front, slip the first st from the RH needle to the LH needle, take the yarn to the back, slip the st back onto the RH needle, then cont.

1st row (wrong side): Knit.
2nd row: K12, turn, k to end.
3rd row: Knit.

4th row: K4, [yo, k2tog] 4 times, yo2, k2tog, k1. (16 sts)
5th row: K3, p1, k12.
6th row: K5, [yo, k2tog] 4 times, yo2, k2tog, k1. (17 sts)
7th row: K3, p1, k13.
8th row: K6, [yo, k2tog] 4 times, yo2, k2tog, k1. (18 sts)
9th row: K3, p1, k14.
10th row: Knit.
11th row: K15, turn, k to end.
12th row: Cast off 3 sts, k14. (15 sts)
Rep these 12 rows.

Garter Stitch Edging

Worked lengthways over 10 sts.

1st row (right side): K3, [yo, k2tog] twice, yo2, k2tog, k1.
(11 sts)

2nd row: K3, p1, k2, [yo, k2tog] twice, k1.

3rd row: K3, [yo, k2tog] twice, k1, yo2, k2tog, k1. (12 sts)

4th row: K3, p1, k3, [yo, k2tog] twice, k1.

5th row: K3, [yo, k2tog] twice, k2, yo2, k2tog, k1. (13 sts)

6th row: K3, p1, k4, [yo, k2tog] twice, k1.

7th row: K3, [yo, k2tog] twice, k6.

8th row: Cast off 3 sts, k4, [yo, k2tog] twice, k1. (10 sts)

Rep these 8 rows.

Picot Braid

Worked lengthways over 5 sts.

Foundation row: Knit.

1st row (right side): Cast on 2 sts, cast off 2 sts, k4.

Rep this 1 row.

Cable Trim

Worked lengthways over 11 sts.

Foundation row: Sl 1, k1, p4, [p in front and back of next st] twice, p1, k2. (13 sts)

1st row (right side): Sl 1, p1, k6, [turn, p3, turn, k3] twice, slip these 3 sts onto cable needle and hold at front, yb, slip 3 sts from RH needle to LH needle, k6, p1, k1.

2nd row: Sl 1, k1, p6, p3 from cable needle, k2.

3rd row: Sl 1, p1, k6, [turn, p3, turn, k3] twice, slip these 3 sts onto cable needle and hold at front, yb, slip 3 sts from LH needle to RH needle, p1, k1.

4th row: Sl 1, k1, p3 from cable needle, p6, k2.

Rep these 4 rows.

Cast off working sl 1, p1, k2, skpo, k1, k2tog, k2, p1, k1 across row. (11 sts)

Leafy Trim

Worked lengthways over 13 sts.

1st row (right side): Sl 1, k2, p2, [k1, yo] twice, k1, p2, k3. (15 sts)

2nd row: Sl 1, k4, p5, k5.

3rd row: Sl 1, k2, p2, k2, yo, k1, yo, k2, p2, k3. (17 sts)

4th row: Sl 1, k4, p7, k5.

5th row: Sl 1, k2, p2, k3, yo, k1, yo, k3, p2, k3. (19 sts)

6th row: Sl 1, k4, p9, k5.

7th row: Sl 1, k2, p2, k4, yo, k1, yo, k4, p2, k3. (21 sts)

8th row: Sl 1, k4, p11, k5.

9th row: Sl 1, k2, p2, k11, p2, k3.

10th row: As 8th row.

11th row: Sl 1, k2, p2, skpo, k7, k2tog, p2, k3. (19 sts)

12th row: As 6th row.

13th row: Sl 1, k2, p2, skpo, k5, k2tog, p2, k3. (17 sts)

14th row: As 4th row.

15th row: Sl 1, k2, p2, skpo, k3, k2tog, p2, k3. (15 sts)

16th row: As 2nd row.

17th row: Sl 1, k2, p2, skpo, k1, k2tog, p2, k3. (13 sts)

18th row: Sl 1, k4, p3, k5.

19th row: Sl 1, k2, p2, M1p, sk2po, M1p, p2, k3.

20th row: Sl 1, k5, p1, k6.

Rep these 20 rows.

Striped Slip Stitch Edging

Worked from bottom edge upwards.

Starts and ends with multiple of 2 sts + 1 st

Note: use three colours of yarn, A, B and C, and strand colours not in use up side of work. Cast on using the cable method and A.

1st row (right side): With A, knit.

2nd row: With A, purl.

3rd row: With B, k1, *sl 1 purlwise, k1; rep from * to end.

4th row: With B, k1, *yf, sl 1 purlwise, yb, k1; rep from * to end.

5th row: With C, knit.

6th row: With C, purl.

7th row: With A, k1, *sl 1 purlwise, k1; rep from * to end.

8th row: With A, k1, * yf, sl 1 purlwise, yb, k1; rep from * to end.

9th row: With B, knit.

10th row: With B, purl.

11th row: With C, k1, *sl 1 purlwise, k1; rep from * to end.

12th row: With C, k1, * yf, sl 1 purlwise, yb, k1; rep from * to end.

13th row: With A, knit.

14th row: With A, purl.

These 14 rows form the edging.

Cast off or cont as required.

Leaf Appliqué

Cast on 3 sts.

1st row (right side): K1 tbl, yo, k1, yo, k1 tbl. (5 sts)

2nd and foll 2 alt rows: P1 tbl, p to last st, p1 tbl.

3rd row: K1 tbl, k1, [yo, k1] twice, k1 tbl. (7 sts)

5th row: K1 tbl, k2, yo, k1, yo, k2, k1 tbl. (9 sts)

7th row: K1 tbl, k3, yo, k1, yo, k3, k1 tbl. (11 sts)

8th and rem alt rows: Purl.

9th row: Ssk, k7, k2tog. (9 sts)

11th row: Ssk, k5, k2tog. (7 sts)

13th row: Ssk, k3, k2tog. (5 sts)

15th row: Ssk, k1, k2tog. (3 sts)

17th row: Sk2po. (1 st)

Fasten off.

Darn in loose ends.

Hearts Braid

Worked from bottom edge upwards.

Starts and ends with multiple of 12 sts + 9 sts.

Note: cast on using the thumb method.

Work 2 rows in garter stitch.

3rd row (right side): P4, k1, *p11, k1; rep from *, ending p4.

4th row: K3, p3, *k9, p3; rep from *, ending k3.

5th row: P3, k3, *p9, k3; rep from *, ending p3.

6th row: K2, p5, *k7, p5; rep from *, ending k2.

7th row: P1, k7, *p5, k7; rep from *, ending p1.

8th row: P9, *k3, p9; rep from * to end.

9th row: K9, *p3, k9; rep from * to end.

10th row: As 8th row.

11th row: K4, p1, *k4, p3, k4, p1; rep from *, ending k4.

12th row: K1, p2, k3, p2, *k5, p2, k3, p2; rep from *, ending k1.

13th row: Purl.

Work 2 rows in garter stitch.

16th row: Purl.

These 16 rows form the edging.

Cast off or cont as required.

Cable Rib

Worked from bottom edge upwards.

Starts and ends with multiple of 10 sts + 6 sts.

Note: cast on using the thumb method.

1st row (right side): *P2, k2, p2, k4; rep from *, ending p2, k2, p2.

2nd row: *K2, p2, k2, p4; rep from *, ending k2, p2, k2.

Rep 1st and 2nd rows once more.

5th row: *P2, k2, p2, C4B; rep from *, ending p2, k2, p2.

6th row: As 2nd row.

Rep these 6 rows once more.

These 12 rows form the edging.

Cast off or cont as required.

Daisy Appliqué

Cast on 6 sts.

1st row (right side): Knit.

2nd row: (K1, p1, k1, p1, k1) in first st, turn, k5, turn, p5, turn, k5, turn, [p2tog] twice, p1, yb, 1 at a time, lift 2nd and 3rd sts over 1st st, yf *p3, turn, sl 1, k3.

3rd row: Purl.

Repeat 1st to 3rd rows 6 more times, then rep 1st row once more and 2nd row to *.

Cast off purlwise.

Join cast on and cast off edges.

Press.

Sew button to centre of flower.

Zigzag Moss Edging

Worked from bottom edge upwards.

Starts and ends with multiple of 6 sts + 1 st.

Note: cast on using the thumb method.

1st row (right side): K1, *p1, k1; rep from * to end.

2nd row: As 1st row.

3rd row: Knit.

4th row: Purl.

5th row: P1, *k5, p1; rep from * to end.

6th row: P1, *k1, p3, k1, p1; rep from * to end.

7th row: P1, *k1, p1; rep from * to end.

8th row: As 7th row.

9th row: K2, p1, k1, p1, *k3, p1, k1, p1; rep from * to last 2 sts, k2.

10th row: P3, k1, *p5, k1; rep from * to last 3 sts, p3.

11th row: Knit.

12th row: Purl.

These 12 rows form the edging.

Cast off or cont as required.

Daisy Braid

Worked lengthways over 12 sts.

1st row (right side): Sl 1, k11.
2nd and 4th rows: Sl 1, k1, p8, k2.
3rd row: Sl 1, k11.
5th row: Sl 1, k3, k2tog, yo2, skpo, k4.
6th row: Sl 1, k1, p3, k1, p4, k2.
7th row: Sl 1, k1, [k2tog, yo2, skpo] twice, k2.

8th row: Sl 1, k1, p1, k1, p3, k1, p2, k2.
9th row: As 5th row.
10th row: As 6th row.
11th row: As 7th row.
12th row: As 8th row.
13th row: As 5th row.
14th row: As 6th row.

Rep these 14 rows, ending with a 3rd row.

Castle Edging

Worked lengthways over 7 sts.

Note: cast on using the cable method.

Work 3 rows in garter st.

4th row (wrong side): Cast on 3 sts, knit all sts. (10 sts)

Work 3 rows in garter st.

8th row: Cast on 3 sts, knit all sts. (13 sts)

9th row: K1, *p1, k1; rep from * to end.

10th row: P1, *k1, p1; rep from * to end.

Rep 9th and 10th rows twice more then 9th row once more.

16th row: Cast off 3 sts knitwise, k to end. (10 sts)

Work 3 rows in garter st.

20th row: Cast off 3 sts knitwise, k to end. (7 sts)

Rep these 20 rows.

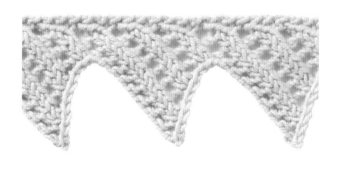

Lace Bunting

Worked lengthways over 4 sts.

Foundation row: K1, yo, k1, p1, k1. (5 sts)

1st and every alt row (wrong side): K2, p to end.

2nd row: K1, yo, k2, p1, k1. (6 sts)

4th row: K1, yo, k1, k2tog, yo, p1, k1. (7 sts)

6th row: K1, yo, k1, k2tog, yo, k1, p1, k1. (8 sts)

8th row: K1, yo, k1, k2tog, yo, k2, p1, k1. (9 sts)

10th row: K1, yo, [k1, k2tog, yo] twice, p1, k1. (10 sts)

12th row: K1, yo, [k1, k2tog, yo] twice, k1, p1, k1. (11 sts)

14th row: K1, yo, [k1, k2tog, yo] twice, k2, p1, k1. (12 sts)

16th row: K1, yo, [k1, k2tog, yo] 3 times, p1, k1. (13 sts)

18th row: Loosely cast off 9 sts, yo, k1, p1, k1. (5 sts)

Rep the 1st to 18th rows.

Fir Cone and Twig Lace

Worked from bottom edge upwards.

Starts and ends with multiple of 10 sts + 1 st.

Note: cast on using the thumb method.

1st row (wrong side): Purl.

2nd row: K1, *yo, k3, sk2po, k3, yo, k1; rep from * to end.

Rep 1st and 2nd rows 3 more times.

9th row: Purl.

10th row: K2tog, *k3, yo, k1, yo, k3, sk2po; rep from * to last 9 sts, k3, yo, k1, yo, k3, skpo.

Rep 9th and 10th rows 3 more times.

These 16 rows form the edging.

Cast off or cont as required.

Rib Stripe Ruffle

Worked from bottom edge upwards.

Starts with multiple of 20 sts + 5 sts.

Ends with multiple of 10 sts + 5 sts.

Note: cast on using the thumb method.

1st row (wrong side): *[P1, k1] twice, p1, k15; rep from *,
ending [p1, k1] twice, p1.

2nd row: *[K1, p1] twice, k1, p15; rep from *, ending
[k1, p1] twice, k1.

Rep 1st and 2nd rows as required, ending with a 2nd row.

Next row (wrong side): *[P1, k1] twice, p1, [k3tog tbl]
5 times; rep from *, ending [p1, k1] twice, p1.

Next row: K1, *p1, k1; rep from * to end.

These rows form the edging.

Cast off or cont as required.

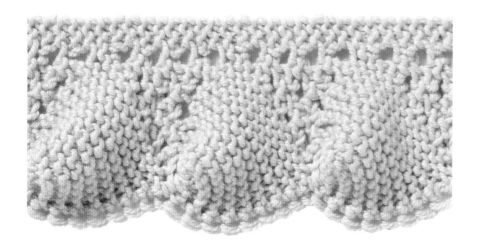

Oyster Shells Lace

Worked lengthways over 16 sts.

1st row (right side): Sl 1, k2, yo2, k13. (18 sts)

2nd row: Yo, k2tog, k12, p1, k3.

3rd row: Sl 1, k to end.

4th row: Yo, k2tog, k16.

5th row: Sl 1, k2, yo2, k2tog, yo2, k13. (21 sts)

6th row: Yo, k2tog, k12, p1, k2, p1, k3.

7th row: As 3rd row.

8th row: Yo, k2tog, k19.

9th row: Sl 1, k2, [yo2, k2tog] 3 times, k12. (24 sts)

10th row: Yo, k2tog, k12, p1, [k2, p1] twice, k3.

11th row: As 3rd row.

12th row: Yo, k2tog, k22.

13th row: Sl 1, k2, [yo2, k2tog] 4 times, k13. (28 sts)

14th row: Yo, k2tog, k13, p1, [k2, p1] 3 times, k3.

15th row: As 3rd row.

16th row: Yo, k2tog, k26.

17th row: Sl 1, k13, sl 1, then, 1 at a time, lift 10 sts over first 2 sts on LH needle, k these 2 sts tog, pass slipped st over, k1. (16 sts)

18th row: Yo, k2tog, k14.

Rep these 18 rows, ending with a 17th row.

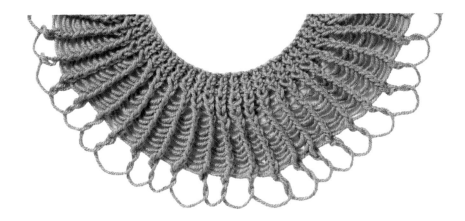

Cobweb Ruffle

Worked from bottom edge upwards.

Starts with multiple of 3 sts + 1 st.

Ends with multiple of 2 sts + 1 st.

Note: cast on using the thumb method.

1st row: K1 tbl, *p2, k1 tbl; rep from * to end.

2nd row: P1, *k1 tbl, k1, p1; rep from * to end.

Rep 1st and 2nd rows 5 more times.

13th row: K1 tbl, *drop next st off needle, p1, k1 tbl; rep from * to end.

14th row: P1, *k1 tbl, p1; rep from * to end.

15th row: K1 tbl, *p1, k1 tbl; rep from* to end.

Rep 14th and 15th rows twice more.

Unravel dropped sts down to cast on edge.

These 19 rows form the edging.

Cast off or cont as required.

Bell Edging 1

Worked from bottom edge upwards.

Starts with multiple of 12 sts + 3 sts.

Ends with multiple of 4 sts + 3 sts.

Note: cast on using the cable method.

1st row (right side): P3, *k9, p3; rep from* to end.

2nd row: K3, *p9, k3; rep from * to end.

3rd row: P3, *yb, skpo, k5, k2tog, p3; rep from * to end.

4th row: K3, *p7, k3; rep from * to end.

5th row: P3, *yb, skpo, k3, k2tog, p3; rep from * to end.

6th row: K3, *p5, k3; rep from * to end.

7th row: P3, *yb, skpo, k1, k2tog, p3; rep from * to end.

8th row: K3, *p3, k3; rep from * to end.

9th row: P3, *yb, sk2po, p3; rep from * to end.

10th row: K3, *p1, k3; rep from * to end.

11th row: P3, *k1, p3; rep from * to end.

12th row: As 10th row.

These 12 rows form the edging.

Cast off or cont as required

Arches Lace

Worked from bottom edge upwards.

Starts and ends with multiple of 11 sts.

Note: cast on using the thumb method.

1st row (right side): *Ssk, k3 tbl, yo, k1, yo, k3 tbl, k2tog; rep from * to end.

2nd and foll 3 alt rows: Purl.

3rd row: *Ssk, k2 tbl, yo, k1, yo, ssk, yo, k2 tbl, k2tog; rep from * to end.

5th row: *Ssk, k1 tbl, yo, k1, [yo, ssk] twice, yo, k1 tbl, k2tog; rep from * to end.

7th row: *Ssk, yo, k1, [yo, ssk] 3 times, yo, k2tog; rep from * to end.

9th row: *K1, p1, k7, p1, k1; rep from * to end.

10th row: *P1, k1, p7, k1, p1; rep from * to end.

Rep 9th and 10th rows once more.

These 12 rows form the edging.

Cast off or cont as required.

Cable Cord

Worked lengthways over 6 sts on double-pointed needles.

1st to 5th rows: Knit, do not turn, slide sts to other end of needle.

6th row: K1, C4F, k1, do not turn, slide sts to other end of needle.

Rep these 6 rows, ending with a 5th row.

Cable and Bobble Braid

Worked lengthways over 5 sts.

Special abbreviation: MB = make bobble. (K1, p1, k1, p1, k1) in next st, then, 1 at a time, lift 2nd, 3rd, 4th and 5th sts over 1st st.

1st foundation row: Knit.

2nd foundation row: Purl.

1st row (right-side): C5B.

2nd and every alt row: Purl.

3rd row: Knit.

5th row: K2, MB, k2.

7th row: Knit.

8th row: Purl.

Rep these 8 rows.

Picot Edging

Worked from bottom edge upwards or top edge downwards.

Starts and ends with multiple of 2 sts + 1 st.

Starting with a k row, work 4 rows st st.

5th row: K1, *yo, k2tog; rep from * to end.

Starting with a p row, work 4 rows st st.

These 9 rows form the edging.

Cont as required

Fold back edging along picot row and slip stitch in place.

Loop Trim

Worked from bottom edge upwards.

Ends with multiple of 12 sts for an odd number of sts and 12 sts + 6 sts for an even number of strips.

Note: Each strip is worked separately and then joined to make loops on one row. Loops can be longer if required.

Cast on 6 sts.

1st row (right side): Sl 1, k5.

2nd row: Sl 1, p5.

Rep 1st and 2nd rows 12 more times.

1st to 26th rows form one strip. Cut yarn and leave strip on needle.

On the same needle, cast on 6 sts and work second strip.

Cont in this way until there are as many strips as required.

Join strips and make loops

Do not cut yarn after completing last strip.

*K6 of first strip, right side facing, position cast on edge of first strip behind second strip, *slip horizontal strand from 1st cast-on st onto LH needle, then k this strand tog with first st of second strip; rep from * for each st.

Cont in this way across strips, ending with k6 from cast on edge of last strip.

Purl 1 row.

These rows form the edging.

Cast off or cont as required.

Openwork Points

Worked lengthways over 7 sts.

1st row (right side): K3, yo, skpo, yo, k2. (8 sts)

2nd and foll 6 alt rows: Sl 1, p to last 2 sts, k2.

3rd row: K4, yo, skpo, yo, k2. (9 sts)

5th row: K5, yo skpo, yo, k2. (10 sts)

7th row: K6, yo, skpo, yo, k2. (11 sts)

9th row: K7, yo, skpo, yo, k2. (12 sts)

11th row: K8, yo, skpo, yo, k2. (13 sts)

13th row: K9, yo, skpo, yo, k2. (14 sts)

15th row: K10, yo, skpo, yo, k2. (15 sts)

16th row: Cast off 8 sts knitwise, p4, k2. (7 sts)

Rep these 16 rows.

Long Loop Fur

Worked from bottom edge upwards.

Starts and ends with multiple of 2 sts + 1 st.

Special abbreviation: ML2 = make double loop. Insert RH needle knitwise into next st, wind yarn over RH needle and around first and second fingers of left hand twice, then over RH needle point once more, draw all 3 loops through st and sl onto LH needle, insert RH needle through back of these 3 loops and original st and k them tog tbl.

Note: Cast on using the cable method. Loops appear on right side rows but are made on wrong side rows.

Work 3 rows in garter stitch.

4th row (wrong side): K1, * ML2, k1; rep from * to end.

Work 3 rows in garter stitch.

8th row: K1, *k1, ML2; rep from * to last 2 sts, k2.

Rep these 8 rows.

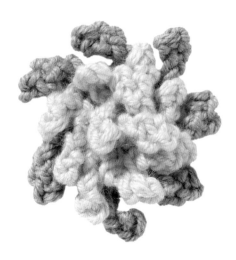

Cast-off Flower Appliqué

Note: two colours of yarn are used, A and B.

With A, cast on 2 sts.

1st row (right side): Knit.

2nd row: Purl.

3rd row: Cast on 6 sts, cast off 6 sts, k1. (2 sts)

4th row: Purl.

Rep 3rd and 4th rows 6 more times.

Change to B.

17th row: Cast on 4 sts, cast off 4 sts, k1. (2 sts)

18th row: Purl.

Rep 17th and 18th rows 11 more times.

Cast off.

Coil up with knit side to inside.

Sew coil together around base.

Beaded Unravelled Fringe

Worked lengthways over any number of sts.

Note: Thread beads onto knitting yarn before casting on, 2 beads for each alt row. First bead is not knitted in.

1st row (right side): K2, slide bead up to back of work, k2, PB, k to end.

2nd row: Purl.

Rep 1st and 2nd rows as required, ending with a 2nd row.

Next row: K3, cast off rem sts.

Slip 3 sts off needle and unravel across knitted fabric to create fringe. Slide 1 bead down to sit at the bottom of each loop.

Bell Edging 2

Worked from upper edge downwards.

Starts with multiple of 8 sts + 7 sts.

Ends with multiple of 20 sts + 7 sts.

1st row (right side): P7, *k1, p7; rep from * to end.

2nd row: K7, *p1, k7; rep from * to end.

3rd row: P7, *yo, k1, yo, p7; rep from * to end.

4th row: K7, *p1 tbl, p1, p1 tbl, k7; rep from * to end.

5th row: P7, *yo, k3, yo, p7; rep from * to end.

6th row: K7, * p1 tbl, p3, p1 tbl, k7; rep from * to end.

7th row: P7, *yo, k5, yo, p7; rep from * to end.

8th row: K7, * p1 tbl, p5, p1 tbl, k7; rep from * to end.

9th row: P7, *yo, k7, yo, p7; rep from * to end.

10th row: K7, * p1 tbl, p7, p1 tbl, k7; rep from * to end.

11th row: P7, *yo, k9, yo, p7; rep from * to end.

12th row: K7, * p1 tbl, p9, p1 tbl, k7; rep from * to end.

13th row: P7, *yo, k11, yo, p7; rep from * to end.

14th row: K7, * p1 tbl, p11, p1 tbl, k7; rep from * to end.

Cast off.

These 14 rows form the edging.

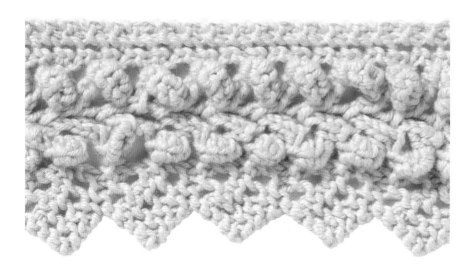

Antique Edging

Worked lengthways over 13 sts.

Note: cast off knitwise throughout.

1st row (right side): K2, yo, skpo, yo, k1, yo, sk2po, yo, k3, yo, k2. (15 sts)

2nd row: K4, [k1, p1] 3 times into next st, p2, k1, p3, k4. (20 sts)

3rd row: K2, yo, skpo, [k1, p1] 3 times into next st, yb, skpo, p1, k2tog, cast off next 5 sts, k to last 2 sts, yo, k2. (19 sts)

4th row: K5, yo, [k1, p1] twice, cast off next 5 sts, k to end. (15 sts)

5th row: K2, yo, skpo, yo, k1, yo, sk2po, yo, k3, yo, k2tog, yo, k2. (17 sts)

6th row: K6, [k1, p1] 3 times into next st, p2, k1, p3, k4. (22 sts)

7th row: K2, yo, skpo, [k1, p1] 3 times into next st, yb, skpo, p1, k2tog, cast off next 5 sts, k to last 4 sts, yo, k2tog, yo, k2. (21 sts)

8th row: Cast off 4 sts, k2, yo, p2, k1, p1, cast off next 5 sts, k to end. (13 sts)

Rep these 8 rows.

Beaded Braid

Worked lengthways over 5 sts.

Note: Thread beads onto knitting yarn before casting on,
3 beads for every 4-row rep.

1st row (right side): Sl 1, k1, PB, k2.
2nd row: Sl 1, p3, k1.
3rd row: Sl 1, [PB, k1] twice.
4th row: As 2nd row.
Rep these 4 rows.

Maypole Lace

Worked lengthways over 26 sts.

Foundation row: Knit.

1st row: Sl 1, k19, [yo, k2tog] twice, yo, k2. (27 sts)

2nd row: K8, p14, k5.

3rd row: Sl 1, k6, [yo, k2tog, k1] 4 times, k2, [yo, k2tog] twice, yo, k2. (28 sts)

4th row: K9, p14, k5.

5th row: Sl 1, k21, [yo, k2tog] twice, yo, k2. (29 sts)

6th row: Knit.

7th row: Sl 1, k4, p14, k4, [yo, k2tog] twice, yo, k2. (30 sts)

8th row: Knit.

9th row: Sl 1, k4, p14, k5, [yo, k2tog] twice, yo, k2. (31 sts)

10th row: Knit.

11th row: Sl 1, k4, p14, k6, [yo, k2tog] twice, yo, k2. (32 sts)

12th row: Cast off 6 sts, k25. (26 sts)

Rep the 1st to 12th rows.

Spiral Rib

Worked from bottom edge upwards.

Starts and ends with multiple of 7 sts.

Note: cast on using the thumb method.

1st row (right side): P2, k4, *p3, k4; rep from * to last st, p1.

2nd row: K1, p3, * k4, p3; rep from * to last 3 sts, k3.

3rd row: P1, k1, p2, *k2, p2, k1, p2; rep from * to last 3 sts, k2, p1.

4th row: K1, p1, k2, p2, *k2, p1, k2, p2; rep from * to last st, k1.

5th row: P1, k3, *p4, k3; rep from * to last 3 sts, p3.

6th row: K2, p4, *k3, p4; rep from * to last st, k1.

7th row: P1, k5, *p2, k5; rep from * to last st, p1.

8th row: K1, p5, *k2, p5; rep from * to last st, k1.

Rep 1st to 8th rows once more.

These 16 rows form the edging.

Cast off or cont as required.

Bobble Rib

Worked from bottom edge upwards.

Starts and ends with multiple of 4 sts + 3 sts.

Special abbreviation: MB = make bobble. (K1, k1 tbl, k1, k1 tbl) in next st, turn, p4, turn, k4, turn, p4, turn, ssk, k2tog, slip 2nd st over 1st st.

Note: cast on using the thumb method.

1st row (right side): P1, *k1, p1; rep from * to end.

2nd and every alt row: K1, *p1, k1; rep from * to end.

3rd row: P1, k1, p1, *MB, p1, k1, p1; rep from * to end.

5th row: As 1st row.

These 5 rows form the edging.

Cast off or cont as required.

Tiny Scallop

Worked lengthways over 5 sts.

1st row (right side): Sl 1, k4.
2nd row: Sl 1, k4.
3rd row: Sl 1, k1, [inc] 3 times. (8 sts)
4th row: Cast off 3 sts, k4. (5 sts)
Rep these 4 rows.

Ruched Edging

Worked from bottom edge upwards.
Starts and ends with multiple of 3 sts.
Note: cast on using the thumb method.

1st row (right side): K2, *sl 1 purlwise, k2; rep from * to last st, k1.
2nd row: P3, *sl 1 purlwise, p2; rep from * to end.
3rd row: K2, *C3F; rep from * to last st, k1.
4th and foll alt row: Purl.
5th row: K2, *yo, k2tog, k1; rep from * to last st, k1.
7th row: K4, *sl 1 purlwise, k2; rep from * to last 2 sts, sl 1 purlwise, k1.
8th row: P1, *sl 1 purlwise, p2; rep from * to last 2 sts, p2.
9th row: K2, *C3B; rep from * to last st, k1.
These 9 rows form the edging.
Cast off or cont as required.

Fan Edging

Worked lengthways over 14 sts.

1st row (wrong side): K2, yo, k2tog, k5, yo, k2tog, yo, k3. (15 sts)

2nd and every alt row: K1, yo, k2tog, k to end.

3rd row: K2, yo, k2tog, k4, [yo, k2tog] twice, yo, k3. (16 sts)

5th row: K2, yo, k2tog, k3, [yo, k2tog] 3 times, yo, k3. (17 sts)

7th row: K2, yo, k2tog, k2, [yo, k2tog] 4 times, yo, k3. (18 sts)

9th row: K2, yo, k2tog, k1, [yo, k2tog] 5 times, yo, k3. (19 sts)

11th row: K2, yo, k2tog, k1, k2tog, [yo, k2tog] 5 times, k2. (18 sts)

13th row: K2, yo, k2tog, k2, k2tog, [yo, k2tog] 4 times, k2. (17 sts)

15th row: K2, yo, k2tog, k3, k2tog, [yo, k2tog] 3 times, k2. (16 sts)

17th row: K2, yo, k2tog, k4, k2tog, [yo, k2tog] twice, k2. (15 sts)

19th row: K2, yo, k2tog, k5, k2tog, yo, k2tog, k2. (14 sts)

20th row: K1, yo, k2tog, k to end.

Rep these 20 rows.

Lace Bells

Worked from bottom edge upwards.

Starts with multiple of 14 sts + 3 sts.

Ends with multiple of 4 sts + 3 sts.

Note: Cast on using the thumb method.

Work 2 rows in garter stitch.

3rd row (right side): P3, *k11, p3; rep from * to end.

4th row: K3, *p11, k3; rep from * to end.

5th row: P3, *yb, skpo, k2, yo, sk2po, yo, k2, k2tog, p3; rep from * to end.

6th row: K3, *p9, k3; rep from * to end.

7th row: P3, *yb, skpo, k1, yo, sk2po, yo, k1, k2tog, p3; rep from * to end.

8th row: K3, *p7, k3; rep from * to end.

9th row: P3, *yb, skpo, yo, sk2po, yo, k2tog, p3; rep from * to end.

10th row: K3, *p5, k3; rep from * to end.

11th row: P3, *yb, skpo, k1, k2tog, p3; rep from * to end.

12th row: K3, *p3, k3; rep from * to end.

13th row: P3, *yb, sk2po, p3; rep from * to end.

14th row: K3, *p1, k3; rep from * to end.

15th row: P3, *k1, p3; rep from * to end.

16th row: As 14th row.

These 16 rows form the edging.

Cast off or cont as required

Laburnum Edging

Worked lengthways over 13 sts.

1st row (right side): K2, yo, p2tog, k1, [yo, skpo] 3 times, yo2, k2tog. (14 sts)

2nd row: P1, k1, p9, yo, p2tog, k1.

3rd row: K2, yo, p2tog, k2, [yo, skpo] 3 times, yo2, k2tog. (15 sts)

4th row: P1, k1, p10, yo, p2tog, k1.

5th row: K2, yo, p2tog, k3, [yo, skpo] 3 times, yo2, k2tog. (16 sts)

6th row: P1, k1, p11, yo, p2tog, k1.

7th row: K2, yo, p2tog, k4, [yo, skpo] 3 times, yo2, k2tog. (17 sts)

8th row: P1, k1, p12, yo, p2tog, k1.

9th row: K2, yo, p2tog, k5, [yo, skpo] 3 times, yo2, k2tog. (18 sts)

10th row: P1, k1, p13, yo, p2tog, k1.

11th row: K2, yo, p2tog, k6, [yo, skpo] 3 times, yo2, k2tog. (19 sts)

12th row: P1, k1, p14, yo, p2tog, k1.

13th row: K2, yo, p2tog, k7, [yo, skpo] 3 times, yo2, k2tog. (20 sts)

14th row: P1, k1, p15, yo, p2tog, k1.

15th row: K2, yo, p2tog, k8, yo, k1, slip last st worked back onto LH needle, then, 1 at a time, lift next 7 sts over this st and off needle, then slip st back onto RH needle. (14 sts)

16th row: P2tog, p9, yo, p2tog, k1. (13 sts)

Rep these 16 rows.

Scallop Shell Lace

Worked from bottom edge upwards.

Starts with multiple of 5 sts + 2 sts.

Ends with multiple of 4 sts + 5 sts.

Note: Cast on using thumb method.

1st row (right side): K1, yo, *k5, 1 at a time, lift the 2nd, 3rd, 4th and 5th sts just worked over the 1st st and off needle, yo; rep from * to last st, k1.

2nd row: P1, *(p1, yo, k1 tbl) into next st, p1; rep from * to end.

3rd row: K2, k1 tbl, *k3, k1 tbl; rep from * to last 2 sts, k2.

Work 3 rows in garter st.

These 6 rows form the edging.

Cast off or cont as required.

Short Loop Fur

Worked from bottom edge upwards.

Starts and ends with multiple of 2 sts + 1 st.

Note: cast on using the cable method. Loops are made and appear on right side rows.

1st row (right side): Knit.

2nd and every alt row: Purl.

3rd row: *K1, ML; rep from * to last st, k1.

5th row: Knit.

7th row: K1, *k1 ML; rep from * to last 2 sts, k2.

8th row: Purl.

Rep these 8 rows.

Parasol Lace

Worked lengthways over 23 sts.

1st row: Sl 1, k2, yo, k1, [p3, k1] 4 times, yo, k3. (25 sts)

2nd and every alt row: Sl 1, k1, p to last 2 sts, k2.

3rd row: Sl 1, k3, yo, k1, [p3, k1] 4 times, yo, k4. (27 sts)

5th row: Sl 1, k4, yo, k1, [p3, k1] 4 times, yo, k5. (29 sts)

7th row: Sl 1, k5, yo, k1, [p2tog, p1, k1] 4 times, yo, k6. (27 sts)

9th row: Sl 1, k6, yo, k1, [p2tog, k1] 4 times, yo, k7. (25 sts)

11th row: Sl 1, k7, yo, k1, [k3tog, k1] twice, yo, k8. (23 sts)

12th row: Sl 1, k1, p to last 2 sts, k2.

Rep these 12 rows.

Two-colour Fringe

Worked lengthways over 12 sts using 1 strand each of
A and B held together.

1st row: K2, yo, k2tog, k1, yo, k2tog, k5.
2nd row: P4, k2, [yo, k2tog, k1] twice.
Rep 1st and 2nd rows as required, ending with a 2nd row.
Next row: Cast off 8 sts and fasten off 9th st.
Slip rem 3 sts off needle and unravel across knitted fabric
to make fringe. Loops can be cut to make single strands.

Layered Tags

Worked from bottom edge upwards.

Starts and ends with multiple of 10 sts.

Note: cast on using the thumb method. Each tag is worked separately and then joined on one row.

Bottom layer

Cast on 10 sts.

1st to 10th rows: Sl 1, k9.

1st to 10th rows form one tag. Cut yarn and leave finished tag on needle. On the same needle, cast on 10 sts and work 2nd tag.

Cont in this way until there are as many tags as required.

Join tags

Do not cut yarn after completing the last tag, but turn and knit across all tags on needle.

Work 7 rows in garter stitch.

Leave sts on spare needle.

Top layer

Cast on 5 sts to make a half-width tag.

1st to 10th rows: Sl1, k4.

Cut yarn and leave sts on needle.

Make full-width tags as for Bottom Layer, making one less tag, and end with another half-width tag.

Join layers

Right side facing, hold top layer in front of bottom layer.

Using 3rd needle, k tog 1 st from each needle across row.

These rows form the edging.

Cast off or cont as required.

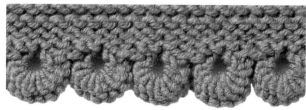

Little Lace

Worked from bottom edge upwards.

Starts and ends with multiple of 9 sts + 4 sts.

Note: cast on using the thumb method.

1st and 3rd rows (wrong side): Purl.

2nd row: K3, *yo, k2, ssk, k2tog, k2, yo, k1; rep from *, ending last rep k2.

4th row: K2, *yo, k2, ssk, k2tog, k2, yo, k1; rep from *, ending last rep k3.

Rep 1st to 4th rows once more.

9th row: Knit.

These 9 rows form the edging.

Cast off or cont as required.

Sugar Scallops

Worked from bottom edge upwards.

Start with multiple of 11 sts + 2 sts.

Ends with multiple of 6 sts + 2 sts.

Note: cast on using the thumb method.

1st row (right side): Purl.

2nd row: K2, *k1, slip this st back onto LH needle, 1 at a time, lift the next 8 sts on LH needle over this st and off needle, yo2, knit the first st again, k2; rep from * to end.

3rd row: K1, *p2tog, drop 1 loop of double yo made in previous row: and [k1, p1] twice into rem loop, p1; rep from * to last st, k1.

Work 5 rows in garter st.

These 8 rows form the edging.

Cast off or cont as required

Star Lace

Worked lengthways over 15 sts.

Foundation row: Knit.

1st row (right side): K3, yo, k3tog, yo, k3, yo, k2tog, [yo2, k2tog] twice. (17 sts)

2nd row: Yo, [k2, p1] twice, k2, yo, k2tog, k7. (18 sts)

3rd row: K3, [yo, k2tog] twice, p1, k2tog, yo, k8.

4th row: K1, cast off 3 sts, k3, p6, k1, yo, k2tog, k1. (15 sts)

5th row: K3, yo, k2tog, k1, yo, k3tog, yo, k2, [yo2, k2tog] twice. (17 sts)

6th row: Yo, [k2, p1] twice, k1, p6, k1, yo, k2tog, k1. (18 sts)

7th row: K3, yo, [k2tog] twice, yo, k1, yo, k2tog, k8.

8th row: K1, cast off 3 sts, k3, p6, k1, yo, k2tog, k1. (15 sts)

Rep the 1st to 8th rows.

Holly Leaf Appliqué

Cast on 3 sts.

1st row (right side): K1 tbl, yo, k1, yo, k1 tbl. (5 sts)

2nd and foll 3 alt rows: P1 tbl, p to last st, p1 tbl.

3rd row: K1 tbl, M1, k1, [yo, k1] twice, M1, k1 tbl. (9 sts)

5th row: K1 tbl, k3, yo, k1, yo, k3, k1 tbl. (11 sts)

7th row: K1 tbl, k4, yo, k1, yo, k4, k1 tbl. (13 sts)

9th row: Cast off 3 sts, k2, yo, k1, yo, k5, k1 tbl. (12 sts)

10th row: Cast off 3 sts, p7, p1 tbl. (9 sts)

11th row: As 5th row. (11 sts)

12th and foll alt row: P1 tbl, p to last st, p1 tbl.

13th row: As 7th row. (13 sts)

15th row: Cast off 3 sts, k8, k1 tbl. (10 sts)

16th row: Cast off 3 sts, p5, p1 tbl. (7 sts)

17th row: Ssk, k3, k2tog. (5 sts)

18th and foll alt row: P1 tbl, p to last st, p1 tbl.

19th row: Ssk, k1, k2tog. (3 sts)

21st row: Sk2po. (1 st)

Fasten off.

Darn in loose ends.

Knots or bobbles can be worked for berries.

Cable and Eyelet Rib

Worked from bottom edge upwards.

Starts and ends with multiple of 7 sts + 3 sts.

Note: cast on using the thumb method.

1st row (right side): P3, *k4, p3; rep from * to end.

2nd row: K1, yo, k2tog, *p4, k1, yo, k2tog; rep from *
to end.

3rd row: P3, *C4B, p3; rep from * to end.

4th row: As 2nd row.

5th row: As 1st row.

6th row: As 2nd row.

Rep 1st to 6th rows once more.

These 12 rows form the edging.

Cast off or cont as required.

Double Knot Edge

Worked lengthways over 8 sts.

1st row (right side): Sl 1, k1, *yo, p2tog, (k1, p1, k1) in next st; rep from * once more. (12 sts)
2nd row: [K3, yo, p2tog] twice, k2.
3rd row: Sl 1, k1, [yo, p2tog, k3] twice.
4th row: Cast off 2 sts knitwise, yo, p2tog, cast off next 2 sts knitwise (4 sts on RH needle), yo, p2tog, k2. (8 sts)
Rep these 4 rows.

Beaded Fringe

Worked lengthways over 5 sts.

Note: Thread beads onto knitting yarn before casting on, 1 bead for each loop.

Special abbreviation: MBL = make bead loop. K1 but do not slip st off LH needle, bring yarn between needles to the front, slide bead up to sit below needles, wind yarn under and over your left thumb, take yarn back between needles to the wrong side, k st on LH needle again ensuring bead remains on loop, then slip second st on RH needle over first st.

1st row (right side): Sl 1, k1, MBL, k2.
2nd row: Sl 1, k4.
3rd and 4th rows: As 2nd row.
Rep these 4 rows.

Lace Diamonds

Worked from bottom edge upwards.

Starts and ends with multiple of 8 sts.

Note: cast on using the thumb method.

1st and every alt row (wrong side): Purl.

2nd row: *K1, yo, k3, pass 3rd st on RH needle over first 2 sts; rep from * to end.

4th row: Knit.

6th row: K3, *yo, skpo, k6; rep from * to last 5 sts, yo, skpo, k3.

8th row: K2, *[yo, skpo] twice, k4; rep from * to last 6 sts, [yo, skpo] twice, k2.

10th row: K1, *[yo, skpo] 3 times, k2; rep from * to last 7 sts, [yo, skpo] 3 times, k1.

12th row: As 8th row.

14th row: As 6th row.

16th row: Knit.

18th row: As 2nd row.

19th row: Purl.

These 19 rows form the edging.

Cast off or cont as required.

Layered Picots

Worked from bottom edge upwards.

Multiple of 3 sts.

Note: two colours of yarn are used, A and B. Use cable cast on throughout. Cast on same number of sts for each layer.

Bottom layer

*Using A, cast on 6 sts, cast off 3 sts, slip st on RH needle onto LH needle, rep from * until required number of stitches are on the LH needle.

1st row (right side): Knit.

2nd row: Purl.

Rep 1st and 2nd rows once more.

Put sts on spare needle.

Top layer

*Using B, cast on 6 sts, cast off 3 sts, slip st on RH needle onto LH needle, rep from * until required number of stitches are on the LH needle.

1st row (wrong side): Purl.

Right side facing, hold top layer in front of bottom layer. Using 3rd needle, k tog 1 st from each needle across row. These rows form the edging.

Cast off or cont as required.

Cable Rope

Worked lengthways over 10 sts.

1st row (wrong side): K2, p6, k2.
2nd row: P2, k6, p2.
3rd row: As 1st row.
4th row: P2, C6B, p2.
5th row: As 1st row.
6th row: P1, T4BR, T4FL, p1.
7th row: K1, p3, k2, p3, k1.
8th row: P1, k3, p2, k3, p1.
Rep 7th and 8th rows 5 more times, then rep 7th row once more.
20th row: P1, T4FL, T4BR, p1.
Rep 1st to 4th rows once more, then rep 1st and 2nd rows once more.
Rep these 26 rows.

Rose Appliqué

Special abbreviation: twist = take the tip of the LH needle under the cast on edge to the back of the work and around to the working position again.
Note: cast on using the thumb method.

Cast on 44 sts.
Starting with a k row, work 3 rows st st.
4th row (wrong side): P4, twist, *p6, twist; rep from * to last 4 sts, p4.
5th row: [K2tog] to end. (22 sts)
6th row: [P2tog] to end. (11 sts)
7th row: [K2tog] to last st, k1. (6 sts)
Cut yarn 15cm from last st. Thread yarn through rem 6 sts and pull up tight.
Join seam.
Sew loops or twists of yarn into centre of flower.

Layered Ruffle

Worked from bottom edge upwards.

Starts with twice the number of sts needed that is an even number. Cast on same number of sts for each layer.

Note: cast on using the thumb method.

Bottom layer

Work 5 rows in garter stitch.

Beg with p row, work 9 rows st st.

15th row (right side): [K2tog] to end.

16th row: Purl.

17th row: Knit.

Place sts on spare needle.

Top Layer

Work 3 rows in garter stitch.

Beg with p row, work 5 rows st st.

9th row (right side): [K2tog] to end.

Join layers

Right side facing, hold top layer in front of bottom layer.

Using 3rd needle, k tog 1 st from each needle across the row.

Work 4 rows in garter stitch.

These rows form the edging.

Cast off or cont as required.

Zigzag Filigree Edging

Worked lengthways over 20 sts.

1st row (right side): K9, [k2tog, yo, k1] 3 times, yo, skpo.

2nd row: Yo, skpo, k18.

3rd row: K8, [k2tog, yo, k1] 3 times, yo, k1, yo, skpo. (21 sts)

4th row: Yo, skpo, yo, skpo, k17.

5th row: K7, [k2tog, yo, k1] 3 times, yo, k1, [yo, skpo] twice. (22 sts)

6th row: Yo, skpo, [yo, skpo] twice, k16.

7th row: K6, [k2tog, yo, k1] 3 times, yo, k1, [yo, skpo] 3 times. (23 sts)

8th row: Yo, skpo, [yo, skpo] 3 times, k15.

9th row: K5, [k2tog, yo, k1] 3 times, yo, k1, [yo, skpo] 4 times. (24 sts)

10th row: Yo, skpo, [yo, skpo] 4 times, k14.

11th row: K4, [k2tog, yo, k1] 3 times, yo, k1, [yo, skpo] 5 times. (25 sts)

12th row: Yo, skpo, [yo, skpo] 5 times, k13.

13th row: K3, [k2tog, yo, k1] 3 times, yo, k1, [yo, skpo] 6 times. (26 sts)

14th row: Yo, skpo, [yo, skpo] 6 times, k12.

15th row: K2, [k2tog, yo, k1] 3 times, yo, k1, [yo, skpo] 7 times. (27 sts)

16th row: Yo, skpo, [yo, skpo] 7 times, k11.

17th row: K4, yo, [k2tog, k1, yo] twice, sk2po, [yo, skpo] 7 times. (26 sts)

18th row: Yo, skpo, [yo, skpo] 6 times, k12.

19th row: K5, yo, [k2tog, k1, yo] twice, sk2po, [yo, skpo] 6 times. (25 sts)

20th row: Yo, skpo, [yo, skpo] 5 times, k13.

21st row: K6, yo, [k2tog, k1, yo] twice, sk2po, [yo, skpo] 5 times. (24 sts)

22nd row: Yo, skpo, [yo, skpo] 4 times, k14.

23rd row: K7, yo, [k2tog, k1, yo] twice, sk2po, [yo, skpo] 4 times. (23 sts)

24th row: Yo, skpo, [yo, skpo] 3 times, k15.

25th row: K8, yo, [k2tog, k1, yo] twice, sk2po, [yo, skpo] 3 times. (22 sts)

26th row: Yo, skpo, [yo, skpo] twice, k16.

27th row: K9, yo, [k2tog, k1, yo] twice, sk2po, [yo, skpo] twice. (21 sts)

28th row: [Yo, skpo] twice, k17.

29th row: K10, yo, [k2tog, k1, yo] twice, sk2po, yo, skpo. (20 sts)

30th row: Yo, skpo, k18.

Rep these 30 rows.

Layered Leaves Braid

Worked lengthways over 18 sts.

1st row (right side): K3, k2tog, yo, k5, yo, k3, skpo, k3.

2nd and every alt row: K3, p12, k3.

3rd row: K3, k2tog, k5, yo, k1, yo, k2, skpo, k3.

5th row: K3, k2tog, k4, yo, k3, yo, k1, skpo, k3.

7th row: K3, k2tog, k3, yo, k5, yo, skpo, k3.

9th row: K3, k2tog, k2, yo, k1, yo, k5, skpo, k3.

11th row: K3, k2tog, k1, yo, k3, yo, k4, skpo, k3.

12th row: As 2nd row.

Rep these 12 rows.

Cockleshells Trim

Worked lengthways over 23 sts.

Work 2 rows in garter stitch

3rd row (right side): K3, yo2, p2tog tbl, k13, p2tog, yo2, k3. (25 sts)

4th row: K4, p1, k15, p1, k4.

Work 2 rows in garter stitch.

7th row: K3, yo2, p2tog tbl, yo2, p2tog tbl, k11, p2tog, yo2, p2tog, yo2, k3. (29 sts)

8th row: K4, p1, k2, p1, k13, p1, k2, p1, k4.

9th row: Knit.

10th row: K7, k15 wrapping yarn 3 times around needle for each st, k7.

11th row: K3, yo2, p2tog tbl, yo2, p2tog tbl, yo2, pass next 15 sts to RH needle dropping extra loops, pass same 15 sts back to LH needle and p all 15 sts tog, yo2, p2tog, yo2, p2tog, yo2, k3. (23 sts)

12th row: K3, p1, [k2, p1] twice, k3, [p1, k2] twice, p1, k3. Rep these 12 rows.

abbreviations

A, B	yarn colours
alt	alternate
beg	begin(s)(ning)
C3B	cable 3 back: slip next 2 stitches onto cable needle, hold at back, knit next stitch, knit 2 stitches from cable needle.
C3F	cable 3 front: slip next stitch onto cable needle, hold at front, knit next 2 stitches, knit stitch from cable needle.
C4(6)B	cable 4(6) back: slip next 2(3) stitches onto cable needle, hold at back, knit next 2(3) stitches, knit 2(3) stitches from cable needle
C4(6)F	cable 4(6) front: slip next 2(3) stitches onto cable needle, hold at back, knit next 2(3) stitches, knit 2(3) stitches from cable needle
C5B	cable 5 back: slip next 3 stitches onto cable needle, hold at back, knit next 2 stitches, knit 3 stitches from cable needle.
cm	centimetre(s)
cont	continue
foll(s)	follow(s)(ing)
in(s)	inch(es)
inc	increase: work into front and back of next stitch
inc2	increase 2: work into front, back and front of next stitch
k	knit
k2tog	knit 2 stitches (or number stated) together
LH	left hand
M1	make one stitch: put tip of left-hand needle under strand between next 2 stitches, lift strand and knit into the back of it.
M1p	make one stitch purl: put tip of left-hand needle under strand between next 2 stitches, lift strand and purl into the back of it.
MB	make bobble: work as instructed in pattern.
ML	make loop: k1 but do not slip st off LH needle, bring yarn between needles to the front, take it under and over your left thumb, take yarn back between needles to the wrong side, k st on LH needle again, then slip second st on RH needle over first st.
P	purl
PB	place bead: bring yarn to front, slide bead up the needle, slip next st purlwise, take yarn to back, tension yarn before working next st.

p2tog	purl 2 stitches (or number stated) together
psso	pass the slipped stitch over
p2sso	pass 2 slipped stitches over
rem	remain(ing)
rep	repeat
rev st st	reverse stocking stitch
RH	right hand
skpo	slip one stitch, knit one stitch, pass slipped stitch over
sk2po	slip one stitch, knit two stitches together, pass slipped stitch over
sl	slip
ssk	slip one stitch, slip one stitch, knit slipped stitches together
st st	stocking stitch
st(s)	stitch(es)
T4B	twist 4 back: slip next 2 stitches onto cable needle, hold at back, knit 2 stitches, purl 2 stitches from cable needle
T4F	twist 4 front: slip next 2 stitches onto cable needle, hold at front, purl 2 stitches, knit 2 stitches from cable needle
T4BR	twist 4 back right: slip next stitch onto cable needle, hold at back, knit next 3 stitches from left-hand needle, purl stitch from cable needle.
T4FL	twist 4 front left: slip next 3 stitches onto cable needle, hold at front, purl next stitch from left-hand needle, knit 3 stitches from cable needle.
tbl	through back of loop
tog	together
WS	wrong side
wyb	with yarn at the back
wyf	with yarn at the front
yb	yarn between needles to back
yf	yarn between needles to front
yo	yarn forward, round or over needle to make a stitch
yo2	yarn forward, round or over needle twice to make 2 stitches
[ ]	rep instruction in square brackets as many times as stated
*	rep instructions following asterisk as many times as stated

index

resources

Rowan
Green Lane Mill
Holmfirth
HD9 2DX
England
www.knitrowan.com

Picture credits:
front cover, 14 Holly Jolliffe
2, 4, 10, 12, 18, Michael Wicks
Istock 6 above right and below left;
9 top row left and right; second row centre; third row left and right;
bottom row centre
All other photography by Geoff Dann
Illustrations by Lotte Oldfield

Publisher's Acknowledgement

We'd like to thank Rowan Yarns for supplying all the yarns used throughout this book. And special thanks to Luise Roberts for all her advice and support.

Other titles currently available in the Harmony Guides series:

KNIT

CROCHET

Love crafts?

Crafters, keep updated on al exciting news from Collins & Brown. Email lovecrafts@anovabooks.com to register for free email alerts and author events.